TOTAL CONSECRATION
THROUGH THE MYSTERIES
OF THE ROSARY

FR. ED BROOM, O.M.V.

TOTAL CONSECRATION

THROUGH THE

MYSTERIES

OF THE

ROSARY

Meditations to Prepare for Total
Consecration to Jesus Through Mary

SOPHIA INSTITUTE PRESS
Manchester, New Hampshire

CONTENTS

ACKNOWLEDGMENTS

I would like to thanks my parents, Mrs. and Mr. Claude Edward Broom; the Oblates of the Virgin Mary; my local community of priests; Fr. Larry Darnell, O.M.V.; and most especially the Virgin Mary for help, support, and inspiration in composing this work of Consecration to Mary — contemplating the Face of Jesus through the eyes and Heart of Mary — hoping that many will love Jesus more and more through Mary.

TOTAL CONSECRATION
THROUGH THE MYSTERIES
OF THE ROSARY

INTRODUCTION

The purpose of our life is to arrive at our final destiny — our home in heaven! God created all of us out of pure love so that we might know Him, love Him, and serve Him in this life and be happy with Him forever in heaven. This is a simple but profound catechetical truth.

To arrive at our destination, heaven, we should carefully plan our route. If we do not, we will drive around like a chicken with its head cut off, as we have all experienced upon getting lost. Many people in the modern world have not the slightest idea where they came from, what their goal in life is, or how to reach that goal. They follow the most current fad, or their feelings, or the advice and suggestions of friends who are even more confused than they are. In the end, sadness and depression invade and permeate their whole being.

Consecration to Mary: the shortcut to heaven

So how do we find our way to heaven? In his masterpiece, *True Devotion to Mary*, Saint Louis Marie de Montfort tells us that the quickest, easiest, shortest, and most efficacious path to Jesus is through the Blessed Virgin Mary. Other paths might lead to union with Jesus eventually, but Mary is the shortcut! Saint Maximilian Kolbe, Pope Saint John Paul II, Saint Bernard, and many other Marian saints have highlighted this all-important truth.

Throughout the Church's history, many have followed this shortcut through various forms of consecration to Jesus through Mary. In these pages, however, we present for your conversion, sanctification, perseverance in grace, and ultimate salvation a new form of consecration—consecration through the Rosary.

Why the Rosary? During each of our Lady's six appearances in Fatima, Portugal, to three children—Lucia de los Santos and Francisco and Jacinta Marto—she insisted on the praying of the Most Holy Rosary. If the Queen of Heaven and Earth, the Mother of Jesus, insisted six times on the daily recitation of the Rosary, it must be of prime importance for our salvation!

Saint John Paul II's devotion to our Lady

Saint John Paul II was shot and almost killed on the feast day of Our Lady of Fatima, May 13, 1981. The following year, on May 13, 1982, he knelt in front of the statue of Our Lady of Fatima, in Portugal. After praying in silence before the statue, the Pope rose and performed a very significant deed: he approached the statue and deposited something in her crown. What was it? Nothing less than the bullet that had been extracted from his body after the attack exactly a year earlier! This bullet can still be found in the crown of the statue of Our Lady of Fatima in Portugal. Saint John Paul II attributed the saving of his life to the powerful intercession of the Blessed Virgin Mary. In his *Witness to Hope: The Biography of Pope John Paul II*, the renowned scholar George Weigel wrote that it was through the mysterious presence of Mary that the bullet was directed in such a way that the Pope was not killed by it.

Evil exists, but our Lady with her power of intercession conquers evil! Consecration to Jesus through Mary will help you triumph over evil.

In his 2002 apostolic letter *The Rosary of the Blessed Virgin Mary*—which all lovers of Mary and the Rosary should read—Saint John Paul II insisted that we pray the Rosary daily, in obedience to the request of Our Lady of Fatima, and for two specific intentions: (1) for world peace (the document was written shortly after the attack on New York's Twin Towers) and (2) for the salvation of the family. And he quoted the famous Rosary priest, Father Patrick Peyton: "The family that prays together, stays together." Father Peyton also said: "A world at prayer is a world at peace."

The Rosary in spiritual warfare

In his classic *Spiritual Exercises*, Saint Ignatius of Loyola includes a powerful meditation entitled "The Two Standards," which considers the constant battle between Satan, who desires our eternal damnation, and Jesus, who desires our eternal salvation. Blessed Bartolo Longo, who is mentioned several times in John Paul II's 2002 letter on the Rosary, embodied the Two Standards. Born and raised a Catholic, he lost his faith while studying at the university, fell into Satanism, and became a priest of Satan. As is to be expected in the lives of those who ally themselves with the Devil, despair soon overwhelmed him. One day, however, Longo heard a gentle but insistent voice: "If you want to be saved, pray the Rosary and propagate the Holy Rosary." This was the voice of the Blessed Virgin Mary, Our Lady of the Rosary! Heeding her advice, Bartolo renounced his practice of Satanism, went to

Confession, and renewed his commitment to his Catholic Faith. In the end, he was instrumental in the construction of one of the most renowned sanctuaries dedicated to Our Lady of the Rosary—Our Lady of Pompeii, near Naples, Italy. Saint John Paul II, Pope Emeritus Benedict XVI, and Pope Francis have all been pilgrims to this extraordinary place.

Bartolo Longo abandoned the Devil's standard for the only sure alternative, Christ and His Church, and embraced the weapon of the Rosary in his spiritual battle. Our spiritual life is likewise warfare—a constant battle against the world, the flesh, and the Devil (see 1 John 2:16)! Therefore, to arrive safe in heaven, we must use our best weapon to conquer our enemy, the Devil, in our short lives here on earth. The young, untrained David in the Old Testament waged war against the experienced fighter Goliath. Yet, with only a sling in hand, he launched at the giant a small stone, which embedded itself in Goliath's brow, and Goliath crashed to the ground. David took the sword of Goliath and cut off his head! Total victory! A sling and a small stone defeated the giant!

We live in perilous times. The Goliaths that surround us, our families, and our children are beyond count! We must enter into mortal battle against them with the help of Jesus and the Blessed Virgin Mary. Our weapon? The Most Holy Rosary! The Rosary is indeed the spiritual sling we must wield daily to defeat Satan and his evil minions.

The method of this new consecration

For all these reasons, the method of this consecration to Jesus through Mary focuses on the Mysteries of the Most Holy Rosary as well as on the Seven Sorrows of Mary. Through this consecration, we will enter into the loving heart of Mary, who willingly suffered with Jesus as Co-Redemptrix. Jesus is the only Redeemer, but our Lady willingly chose to suffer most intensely with Jesus, especially beneath the Cross, for the salvation of the entire world—and that includes you and me.

Daily Meditation

The program lasts five weeks. Each day you will be invited to meditate on one of the Mysteries of the Most Holy Rosary. Set aside a time (if possible, the earlier in the day, the better) and find a place where you can be alone in silence with Jesus and Mary and enter into profound communion and dialogue with them.

Begin by begging the Holy Spirit and Mary for the grace to pray well. Next contemplate a picture of Mary. Then read the biblical passage for the day and the running commentary on it. As Saint Ignatius teaches us, when some passage, word, or idea strikes you, stop and pray over that point or idea (this is the movement of the Holy Spirit), and stay with it as long as fervor remains! When you become distracted, return to your reading and meditation.

Revisions

After you have finished your daily encounter with Jesus and Mary, reflect on how it spoke to you. Then take a few minutes to write down your revision—how Jesus and Mary spoke to you, what personal message Jesus and Mary gave you in your prayer time. (If this program is done in a group setting, you will be invited to share one of these meditations in a small group with the help of a facilitator.)

Consecration

As with Saint Louis de Montfort's consecration, aim to begin this program about five weeks before a Marian feast, so that you can consecrate yourself to Jesus through Mary on that feast day. Here are some feast days from which you may choose:

- The Immaculate Conception of the Blessed Virgin Mary: December 8

- Our Lady of Guadalupe: December 12

- The Nativity of Our Lord: December 25

- Mary, the Holy Mother of God: January 1

- Our Lady of Lourdes: February 11

- The Annunciation of the Lord: March 25, or another date if March 25 falls during Holy Week

- Our Lady of Fatima: May 13

- The Visitation of the Blessed Virgin Mary: May 31

- The Immaculate Heart of the Blessed Virgin Mary: movable feast that falls twenty days after Pentecost

- Our Lady of Mount Carmel: July 16

- The Assumption of the Blessed Virgin Mary: August 15

- The Queenship of the Blessed Virgin Mary: August 22

- The Nativity of the Blessed Virgin Mary: September 8

- The Most Holy Name of Mary: September 12

- Our Lady of Sorrows: September 15

- Our Lady of the Rosary: October 7

- The Presentation of the Blessed Virgin Mary: November 21

Then, every year on that feast, renew your consecration to Jesus through Mary and go deeper and deeper into the infinite abyss of the love of Mary your Mother.

The External Sign of Your Consecration

The external sign of your consecration to Jesus through Mary is the Brown Scapular of Our Lady of Mount Carmel. This is the garment of Mary, to be worn as a sign that you belong to her — that you are in the school of Mary, in the family of Mary, and in the Immaculate Heart of Mary. Obtain a Brown Scapular at a religious-goods store or online, and on the day of your consecration, ask a priest to enroll you in the Brown Scapular. Wear it always as a sign of your belonging to Jesus though Mary, a sign of your living constantly in the loving Immaculate Heart of Mary, your place of rest, your solace, your refuge. Kiss your Scapular every morning as you renew your consecration to Mary, and kiss it each night before you go to sleep.

Meditation Steps

- *Place yourself in the presence of God.* Imagine that God is looking into your eyes with great love.

- *Pray to the Holy Spirit.* Ask the Holy Spirit to teach you how to pray. "Come, Holy Spirit, come to me through the Immaculate Heart of Mary."

- *Ask Mary to pray with you and for you.* She will never fail to help you to go deep in your meditations.

- *Read the text.* Stop where God seems to be moving you.

- *Distractions?* Read the text again. When God seems to be speaking to you, stop and enter into conversation with Him.

- *Colloquy.* Do a single, double, or triple colloquy:
    Talk to Mary and then pray the Hail Mary.
    Talk to Jesus and then pray the Soul of Christ prayer (below).
    Talk with the Eternal Father and then pray the Our Father.
    Finally, talk to the Holy Spirit and then pray the Holy Spirit prayer (facing page).

Soul of Christ (Anima Christi)

Soul of Christ, sanctify me.
Body of Christ, save me.
Blood of Christ, inebriate me.

Introduction

Water from the side of Christ, wash me.
Passion of Christ, strengthen me.
O good Jesus, hear me.
Within Your wounds, hide me.
Suffer me not to be separated from You.
From the malignant enemy, defend me.
At the hour of death, call me.
And bid me come to You.
That with Your saints I may praise You.
Forever and ever. Amen.

St. Augustine's Holy Spirit Prayer

Breathe in me, O Holy Spirit,
That my thoughts may all be holy.
Act in me, O Holy Spirit,
That my work, too, may be holy.
Draw my heart, O Holy Spirit,
That I love only what is holy.
Strengthen me, O Holy Spirit,
To defend all that is holy.
Guard me, then, O Holy Spirit,
That I always may be holy. Amen.

Week 1

THE JOYFUL MYSTERIES

Day 1: First Joyful Mystery

The Annunciation of the Angel Gabriel to the Blessed Virgin Mary

---

Luke 1:26–38
Read slowly and prayerfully

In the sixth month the angel Gabriel was sent from God to a city of Galilee named Nazareth, to a virgin betrothed to a man whose name was Joseph, of the house of David; and the virgin's name was Mary. And he came to her and said, "Hail, full of grace, the Lord is with you!" But she was greatly troubled at the saying, and considered in her mind what sort of greeting this might be. And the angel said to her, "Do not be afraid, Mary, for you have found favor with God. And behold, you will conceive in your womb and bear a son, and you shall call his name Jesus.

He will be great, and will be called the Son of the Most
    High;
and the Lord God will give to him the throne of his
    father David,
and he will reign over the house of Jacob for ever;
and of his kingdom there will be no end."

And Mary said to the angel, "How can this be, since I have no husband?" And the angel said to her,
"The Holy Spirit will come upon you,
and the power of the Most High will overshadow you;
therefore the child to be born will be called holy,
the Son of God.
And behold, your kinswoman Elizabeth in her old age has also conceived a son; and this is the sixth month with her who was called barren. For with God nothing will be impossible." And Mary said, "Behold, I am the handmaid of the Lord; let it be to me according to your word." And the angel departed from her.

Meditate on the Annunciation

Our first parents, Adam and Eve, committed the first sin, known as Original Sin. To punish Adam and Eve, God banished them from Eden and closed the gates of heaven to them and to their offspring. God's mercy exceeds His justice, however, so over the course of many centuries He sent prophets to prepare His people to receive the Redeemer He would send to save the world and its people from sin. At last God blessed a holy couple named Joachim and Anne with a child: the Virgin Mary, who was destined from all eternity to give birth to our Savior, the Lord Jesus Christ.

Mary was all beautiful in the eyes of God. Unlike any of us, she was conceived without Original Sin, and never in her life did she sin. She is immaculate — the sinless one: humble, sincere, pure, and innocent.

Mary made a vow of virginity so that she could give her whole self to God — her body, mind, heart, and soul. Total consecration to God enabled her to love silence so that she could listen to

God and enabled her to love to talk to God and to do His holy will. Total consecration to Jesus through Mary will help you to do the same.

Consider thoughtfully

Mary's Silence

The Gospels emphasize Mary's silence, telling us that, instead of running about telling others about the things that happened to her, "Mary pondered all things in her heart" (Luke 2:19). St. Ambrose adds that "this holy Virgin always carried in the depths of her heart the mysteries of God and the Passion of her son and whatever else He did." Such mindfulness is impossible without the silence that alone protects and preserves it. Silence enables us to listen; listening enables us to hear; and hearing the voice of God invites us to respond to Him — *all of which is prayer.*

Do this now: Consider Mary's silence and ask her to help you find some time in your busy day to be silent. From your daily silence will come listening to God, and from listening will come prayer.

Mary's Purity

Jesus said: "Blessed are the pure of heart for they will see God" (Matt. 5:8). Mary is pure in body, mind, soul, spirit, and intention. Like Mary we are called to live lives of great purity, and consecration to Mary can help us to do so. If you have lost your purity, Mary's prayers and powerful intercession will help you recover it so that you will once again be pleasing to God.

Do this now: Ask Mary to help you control your eyes, your thoughts, your imagination, your feelings, your actions, and even your intentions. Like her, seek to do all for the honor and glory of God!

The Angel's Annunciation

Gabriel means "Power of God," and his arrival in Nazareth presages one of God's most powerful deeds: the Incarnation of Jesus. Gabriel greets Mary with the words "Hail Mary, full of grace." We lose grace through mortal sin and recover it through a good sacramental confession. Mary never lost grace but preserved it through her constant love of God.

Do this now: In preparation for your consecration (and every day hereafter), ask Mary to help you preserve grace in your soul or to recover it through repentance. Resolve to go regularly to confession and to undertake your penance with gratitude and joy.

How Can This Be?

The angel announces good news: Mary will conceive a Child whose name will be Jesus. He will free the people from their sins. Mary, however, wants to be faithful to her promise to God, her vow of virginity, so she asks for clarification. She wants to be true to her promise as you must be to yours.

Do this now: Resolve ever to be honest and faithful to the promises that you make to God and to others, particularly as you prepare yourself for consecration to Jesus through Mary. Go carefully, as did Mary, when circumstances seem to call for you to break promises or to violate vows.

Cousin Elizabeth's Pregnancy

The sign that God gives Mary through the archangel Gabriel is that Mary's cousin Elizabeth, who had been barren, has conceived a child in her old age. In fact, she is already in her sixth month. Nothing is impossible for God!

> *Do this now*: Imagine and share in the joy that Mary must have experienced at this good news about her cousin who suffered so many years because she could not have a baby. Talk to Mary about it, and thank her for the little "miracles" that have happened in your life.

Mary's Yes Transforms the World

Upon hearing of this good news, this miracle, Mary joyfully responds to the angel by saying yes to God: "Behold, I am the handmaid of the Lord; let it be to me according to your word" (Luke 1:38). Mary's yes to God results in the Incarnation of the Son of God—in the descent of the Second Person of the Blessed Trinity from heaven to earth. Mary's yes to God changed the world for all time; in fact, her yes redounds to eternity!

> *Do this now*: Resolve always to say yes to God, in things small and in large. Your yes will change the world around you.

The Virginal Conception

Immediately after consenting to the Incarnation, Mary is overshadowed by the Holy Spirit, and she conceives Jesus in her most pure and immaculate womb. In this way, Mary is able to remain faithful to her promise and vow to God—namely, to keep her beautiful vow of virginity of mind, heart, body, and soul. Mary's heart is filled with joy because she said yes to God and yes to the salvation of the entire human race.

> *Do this now*: Imagine the joy that Mary must have felt in learning that she was so pleasing to God. Imagine her even greater joy at the news that the long-promised Messiah was

finally being sent. Thank God for choosing Mary as His instrument and even more for condescending to send His Son to save us from our sins.

Finally, talk with Mary

As you prepare to consecrate yourself to Jesus through Mary, reflect seriously upon this profound mystery of the Annunciation of the archangel Gabriel that resulted in the Incarnation. Talk about it to Mary as a child speaks to his Mother. Thank her for her yes to God that brought salvation to mankind. Ask her to help you imitate her silence, her purity, and her generosity, and to love her. Soon, you will experience the true joy and happiness that Mary felt and that comes to all who overcome their selfishness and learn to give themselves totally to God.

THE VISITATION OF MARY TO HER COUSIN ELIZABETH

Luke 1:39–56
Read slowly and prayerfully

In those days Mary arose and went with haste into the hill country, to a city of Judah, and she entered the house of Zechariah and greeted Elizabeth. And when Elizabeth heard the greeting of Mary, the babe leaped in her womb; and Elizabeth was filled with the Holy Spirit and she exclaimed with a loud cry, "Blessed are you among women, and blessed is the fruit of your womb! And why is this granted me, that the mother of my Lord should come to me? For behold, when the voice of your greeting came to my ears, the babe in my womb leaped for joy. And blessed is she who believed that there would be a fulfilment of what was spoken to her from the Lord." And Mary said,

"My soul magnifies the Lord,
and my spirit rejoices in God my Savior,
for he has regarded the low estate of his handmaiden.
For behold, henceforth all generations will call me
    blessed;

for he who is mighty has done great things for me,
and holy is his name.
And his mercy is on those who fear him
from generation to generation.
He has shown strength with his arm,
he has scattered the proud in the imagination of their
    hearts,
he has put down the mighty from their thrones,
and exalted those of low degree;
he has filled the hungry with good things,
and the rich he has sent empty away.
He has helped his servant Israel,
in remembrance of his mercy,
as he spoke to our fathers,
to Abraham and to his posterity for ever."

And Mary remained with her about three months, and returned to her home.

Meditate on the Visitation

Mary's cousin has suffered for many years because she could not have a child. Now in her old age she is pregnant. Soon after Mary learns this remarkable fact from the archangel Gabriel, she resolves to help her elderly cousin with her pregnancy, even though that will require Mary to walk ninety miles to Ein Karem where Elizabeth lives.

After a long, tiring, but joyful journey, Mary arrives at the home of Elizabeth. It's obviously a surprise visit! With overflowing joy, Mary greets Elizabeth: "Shalom!" they both cry: "Peace be with you!"

Mary's total devotion to God gave her the strength and the will to serve others however and whenever she could, not counting the cost to herself. Total consecration to Jesus through Mary will help you do the same.

Consider thoughtfully

Mary Starts Her Journey

Mary, filled with the Holy Spirit and carrying Jesus in her womb, immediately begins her journey. She moves in haste. When it comes to acts of love and service, she doesn't procrastinate or wait until tomorrow. She begins today.

Do this now: Like Mary, resolve not to ignore or delay acting on your genuine good inspirations. Carry them out promptly ... and joyfully!

Eucharistic Marian Processions

Because Mary carries Jesus in her womb as she travels to Ein Karem, in a very real sense her journey is the very first Eucharistic-Marian procession. As you travel with Mary in spirit, then, you, too, are taking part in a Eucharistic-Marian procession.

Do this now: When you are weary and the road seems too long, remember Mary and Jesus in her womb on the road to Elizabeth's house in Ein Karem. Tell Mary that now you understand better what she suffered—and what Jesus will suffer when He bears His Cross—and resolve to bear your difficulties with patience and good-heartedness, as they bore theirs. The more you do this with Mary's trip in mind, the more you will grow in love for Jesus in the Eucharist.

Elizabeth's Baby Leaps for Joy

When Mary greets Elizabeth, the baby in Elizabeth's womb (who will grow up to be the great Saint John the Baptist) leaps with joy! Elizabeth exclaims: "Blessed are you among women, and blessed is the fruit of your womb! And why is this granted me, that the mother of my Lord should come to me?" (Luke 1:42–44).

Do this now: Now is the time for you, too, to rejoice with these two pregnant, joyful mothers. Despite their difficulties, they rejoice and trust all the more in God and His divine providence, knowing that He is good and will reward their faithfulness. Ask Mary to bless you and your children and to fill you with great faith, love, and trust in God!

Mary's Canticle of Praise

In response to Elizabeth's greeting—"Blessed are you among women …"—from Mary's Immaculate Heart springs a hymn of praise, which we call the Magnificat.

Do this now: Join now with Mary in praising God by praying the Magnificat:

My soul magnifies the Lord,
and my spirit rejoices in God my Savior,
for he has regarded the low estate of his handmaiden.
For behold, henceforth all generations will call me
    blessed;
for he who is mighty has done great things for me,
and holy is his name.
And his mercy is on those who fear him
from generation to generation.
He has shown strength with his arm,

he has scattered the proud in the imagination of their
  hearts,
he has put down the mighty from their thrones,
and exalted those of low degree;
he has filled the hungry with good things,
and the rich he has sent empty away.
He has helped his servant Israel,
in remembrance of his mercy,
as he spoke to our fathers,
to Abraham and to his posterity for ever

Mary's Three Months with Elizabeth

In those days, household labor was arduous. In that arid land, dust and dirt got into everything. Merely keeping things clean was difficult. There were no vacuum cleaners, washing machines, or dryers. In fact, there was no running water: Elizabeth and Mary had to walk to the town well to draw water for cooking and cleaning. In your mind, work alongside Mary as she helps elderly Elizabeth and her husband, Zechariah.

♦ *Drawing water*: Accompany Mary to the well to draw water. Walk with her and be with her as she waits until it is her turn. Help Mary to lower the bucket to the depths to draw out water that will be used in cooking, cleaning, and washing in the course of the day. Ask our Lady to obtain for you living water—the Holy Spirit.

♦ *Washing and cleaning*: Mary has to wash the clothes by hand and lay them out to dry. Be with her and help her. Beg her to help you cleanse your soul from the moral guilt that we call sin. As you do so, ask her to help you clean your home as well—physically, morally, and spiritually.

- *Cooking*: As Mary prepares meals for the elderly couple, ask for her help as you prepare meals for your family. Remember, however, that "man does not live by bread alone," and try to nourish your family spiritually in all that you say and do, always seeking Mary's help. And remember that silence with good works is sometimes more eloquent than preaching.

- *Meals together*: Not every moment is consumed by work. Imagine Mary after dinner, after having prepared the meal and set the table. She is seated with Elizabeth and Zechariah. Imagine the conversation of the three, or rather *four*, because you are there. Listen attentively, and then enter into the conversation. Your conversation and interaction is very important to Mary. After the meal, be ready and willing to help Mary clean up.

- *Prayer together*: A very important part of Mary's visit was spiritual encouragement for her elderly, pregnant cousin. Imagine the prayer time they must have shared together. The psalms, canticles, songs, prayers of praise and supplication, as well as prayers of thanksgiving—all of these would have been part of this simple but profound time of prayer. Listen to them pray, and do not be afraid to add your own prayers that surge from the depths of your heart. Mary is very interested in your prayers!

- *Conversations*: Apart from prayer and work, Mary spent time simply talking with Elizabeth in deep friendship. Imagine what they must have said to each other. Now enter into conversation with them. Tell them about your concerns, and your hopes and fears. And tell them about your coming consecration to Jesus through Mary.

Finally, walk with Mary daily

In the days of her pregnancy, Mary rejoices in the baby Jesus in her womb, but she also rejoices in having you at her side as she walks and works alongside Elizabeth! From today forward, as you prepare to consecrate yourself to Jesus through Mary, and for the rest of your life, walk and work side by side with Mary, and with Jesus, who is in her womb. Let your whole life become a Eucharistic-Marian procession.

As you go through your day, talk to Mary about who you are, what is going on in your life, what is on your mind and bothering you, and what you fear or worry about. Tell her about your goals and projects. Listen to what she wants to say to you. Joy will flood your life as you come to know Jesus and Mary better by spending time daily with them. Close each conversation with a fervent Hail Mary.

THE BIRTH OF JESUS, THE SON OF MARY

Luke 2:1–20
Read slowly and prayerfully

In those days a decree went out from Caesar Augustus that all the world should be enrolled. This was the first enrollment, when Quirinius was governor of Syria. And all went to be enrolled, each to his own city. And Joseph also went up from Galilee, from the city of Nazareth, to Judea, to the city of David, which is called Bethlehem, because he was of the house and lineage of David, to be enrolled with Mary, his betrothed, who was with child. And while they were there, the time came for her to be delivered. And she gave birth to her first-born son and wrapped him in swaddling cloths, and laid him in a manger, because there was no place for them in the inn.

And in that region there were shepherds out in the field, keeping watch over their flock by night. And an angel of the Lord appeared to them, and the glory of the Lord shone around them, and they were filled with fear. And the angel said to them, "Be not afraid; for behold, I bring you good news of a great joy which will come to all the people; for to you is born this day in the city of David a Savior, who is Christ the Lord. And this will be a sign for you: you will find a babe wrapped in swaddling cloths and lying in a manger." And suddenly there was with the angel a multitude of the heavenly host praising God and saying,

"Glory to God in the highest,
and on earth peace among men with whom he is
pleased!"

When the angels went away from them into heaven, the shepherds said to one another, "Let us go over to Bethlehem and see this thing that has happened, which the Lord has made known to us." And they went with haste, and found Mary and Joseph, and the babe lying in a manger. And when they saw it they made known the saying which had been told them concerning this child; and all who heard it wondered at what the shepherds told them. But Mary kept all these things, pondering them in her heart. And the shepherds returned, glorifying and praising God for all they had heard and seen, as it had been told them.

Meditate on the Birth of Jesus

Every year we celebrate the most important birthday in the history of the world—that of Our Lord and Savior Jesus Christ. This birth changed the course of history and the face of the earth.

What a contrast there is, however, between the coziness and the rich fare of our Christmas celebrations and the conditions in which Christ's birth took place.

Join Saint Ignatius of Loyola in his devotion to *La Madonna de la Strada*—Our Lady of the Way: imagine that you are traveling with the Holy Family to Bethlehem. Mary likely rode on a donkey most of the way, with Joseph walking beside her. Nonetheless, for Mary, on the verge of giving birth, it was a long, arduous journey.

Finally, they arrive in Bethlehem, but the circumstances do not get better. They are tired, hungry, and exhausted from their journey, and although Joseph seeks to provide shelter for his family, none can be found. Imagine this poor man knocking on doors and seeking a room at least for that one night. But there is no room for them, and they have to take shelter for the night in a stable, where Mary will soon give birth to the Savior of the universe.

Let us reflect on these events in order to get to know Jesus, Mary, and Joseph better. Through that knowledge our lives will be transformed.

Consider thoughtfully

Joy amid Hardship

Even though the journey from Nazareth to Bethlehem is long and painful, it is bathed in joy! Why? Jesus is with Mary and Joseph during the whole journey. In the hardships of your life's journey, you, too, can experience joy. But to do so, you must journey with Jesus, Mary, and Joseph, trusting all the while in God's loving providence—therein lies the secret to true and lasting joy.

Do this now: Ask our Lady to accompany you in every step along your journey to heaven. She longs to talk to you, to be with you, and to encourage you! Talk to Mary and beg her for the grace to imitate her. Beg her for greater trust in God's providence. Implore her for greater detachment from the things of this world so that your heart can be totally attached to Jesus, as was Mary's Immaculate Heart!

The Cold and the Wind
Imagine the cold nights, the howling winds, and the rocky paths that the Holy Family encounter on their journey. Yet they persevere despite inclement weather and rough pathways.

Do this now: Beg our Lady for the gift of perseverance, especially in your prayer life in the midst of life's many storms.

No Room at the Inn
Rejection is painful. Instead of growing angry, resentful, or bitter about it, Mary and Joseph humbly accept it. Have you ever been rejected by anybody? What was your reaction? Maybe you are still holding on to resentment, and bitterness is still festering in your heart, preventing both peace and joy from reigning there.

Do this now: One of our Lady's titles is Health of the Sick. Talk to her about rejections you have suffered and beg her to implore Jesus to heal your mind, your heart, and your soul.

The Stable of Bethlehem
They must pass the night in a stable adjoining a shallow cave where animals shelter against the rain and the wind. The ground is rocky and hard. The smell? Not agreeable, to say the least—the smell of barn animals and manure. The only furnishing is a manger—a wooden trough filled with straw to feed the animals.

Joseph and Mary don't complain, but gratefully accept these modest "lodgings" as the will of God for them and for the Child who is about to be born.

Do this now: The stable is dark and cold. Help Joseph gather sticks and straw to make a fire for Mary and Jesus. Marvel at his patience while he does so, and at his love for Mary and the baby. Turn to our Lady, who still has the unborn baby Jesus warmly cuddled in her most pure womb. She wants to hold you, too, in her arms and in her Immaculate Heart. Ask her to implore Jesus to draw you close to Her; beg her to give you the grace to accept fully and completely God's will in your life—this is the key to joy and peace!

Jesus Is Born

In the midst of this extreme poverty, in the middle of the night, one of the most wonderful and extraordinary things happens. Jesus, the Son of the Eternal Father, is born of the Blessed Virgin Mary. Without losing the splendor of her virginity, Mary brings forth Jesus, the Savior of the world. Small, tender, and vulnerable, the newborn Jesus is totally dependent on Mary and on Saint Joseph, His foster father.

Do this now: Contemplate with great love this most tender scene. All this happened for love of you and me. Our Lady rejoices in your great love for Jesus. Look into her eyes and ask her to give you the Infant Jesus. Our Lady is happy to allow you to hold and love Jesus as long as your heart desires! In your imagination take Him into your arms, kiss Him, and love Him.

Bethlehem: The House of Bread

Jesus was born of the Blessed Virgin Mary in Bethlehem, which means "the House of Bread." Later, in His public life, Jesus calls Himself "the Bread of Life." Just as the Bread of Life was formed in the womb of Mary, so our Lady wants to help form you into another Jesus.

Do this now: Beg our Lady for the grace to be able to receive Jesus, the Bread of Life, often in Holy Communion, but always with great love and devotion. Pray that you will soon be able to join Saint Paul in saying, "It is no longer I who live, but Christ who lives in me" (Gal. 2:20).

Finally, enter into deep conversation with Mary

Speak to Mary about the Birth of Jesus in Bethlehem. Mary said yes to God and brought forth Jesus in Bethlehem for love of you and for the sake of your eternal salvation. Thank her! Love Mary and beg her for all the graces that you will need as you consecrate yourself to Jesus through her. Do not hesitate and do not be afraid. She longs to help you abundantly and right now!

Day 4: Fourth Joyful Mystery

THE PRESENTATION OF THE CHILD JESUS IN THE TEMPLE

Luke 2:22–40
Read slowly and prayerfully

And when the time came for their purification according to the law of Moses, they brought him up to Jerusalem to present him to the Lord (as it is written in the law of the Lord, "Every male that opens the womb shall be called holy to the Lord") and to offer a sacrifice according to what is said in the law of the Lord, "a pair of turtledoves, or two young pigeons." Now there was a man in Jerusalem, whose name was Simeon, and this man was righteous and devout, looking for the consolation of Israel, and the Holy Spirit was upon him. And it had been revealed to him by the Holy Spirit that he should not see death before he had seen the Lord's Christ. And inspired by the Spirit he came into the temple; and when the parents brought in the child Jesus, to do for him according to the custom of the law, he took him up in his arms and blessed God and said,

"Lord, now lettest thou thy servant depart in peace,
according to thy word;

for mine eyes have seen thy salvation
which thou hast prepared in the presence of all peoples,
a light for revelation to the Gentiles,
and for glory to thy people Israel."
And his father and his mother marveled at what was
    said about him; and Simeon blessed them and said
    to Mary his mother,
"Behold, this child is set for the fall and rising of many
    in Israel,
and for a sign that is spoken against
(and a sword will pierce through your own soul also),
that thoughts out of many hearts may be revealed."
And there was a prophetess, Anna, the daughter of Phanuel, of the tribe of Asher; she was of a great age, having lived with her husband seven years from her virginity, and as a widow till she was eighty-four. She did not depart from the Temple, worshiping with fasting and prayer night and day. And coming up at that very hour she gave thanks to God, and spoke of him to all who were looking for the redemption of Jerusalem.

And when they had performed everything according to the law of the Lord, they returned into Galilee, to their own city, Nazareth. And the child grew and became strong, filled with wisdom; and the favor of God was upon him.

Meditate on the Presentation

Mary and Saint Joseph travel to Jerusalem to present the Infant Jesus in the Temple. There is joy in this trip, because the Holy Family is united in their love for God and their desire to carry out God's holy will. When they arrive in Jerusalem — the City of Peace — they carry Jesus, barely six weeks old, to the majestic Temple of Jerusalem, which was built by order of King Solomon, the son of King David.

But in a very real sense, the Temple of Jerusalem is the second Temple that Jesus has entered: the first was our Lady, the temple and resting place of our Lord during the nine months of her pregnancy — a temple more beautiful than the majestic Temple of Jerusalem.

The Temple of Jerusalem contains the *symbolic presence* of God; our Lady contained within her womb the *Real Presence* of God. With what love and tenderness did our Lady cherish Jesus in her womb, and when He was born, how much love and tenderness does she shower upon Him, her greatest treasure.

Yet at the Temple of Jerusalem, a shadow falls on Mary, the temple of Jesus: Simeon foretells Jesus' Passion, suffering, and death, the sword that will penetrate Mary's heart as the centurion's sword will penetrate Jesus' side.

Consider thoughtfully

Saint Joseph the Protector

The first lover of Jesus and Mary was good Saint Joseph, who was called by God the Father to be the husband of the Virgin Mary. Even more important, Saint Joseph was called to be the foster father of Jesus. His was the most sublime role in the world after those of Mary and Jesus. How he must have suffered when he heard the chilling prophecy of Simeon!

Do this now: Talk to Saint Joseph as if he were your spiritual father. He cares for you; he loves you; he can attain for you many choice graces; and he can bring you to a

deeper knowledge of, love for, and union with Mary and
Jesus.

You as a Temple

The moment you were baptized, you became a temple of the
Living God: the Father, the Son, and the Holy Spirit. Through
your Baptism you have become a son or daughter of God the
Father, a brother or sister of Jesus Christ, and an intimate friend
of the Holy Spirit.

> *Do this now*: Beg our Lady to help you recognize your great
> dignity as well as your eternal destiny—which is none
> other than to be with our Lady in heaven to glorify the
> Trinity for all eternity.

The Prophet Simeon

The eyes of the elderly mystic Simeon perceived Jesus in the
arms of our Lady. He rejoiced exultantly and praised God, for
finally the day had arrived not only to see Jesus, the Son of
Mary, but to hold Jesus in his arms. Now Simeon is ready to go
in peace—even to die if this is God's will—because his eyes
have finally beheld the promised One of Israel. Now you, too,
should rejoice because you have an even greater privilege than
Simeon. In Mass, in the Consecration, and in the exposition
of the Blessed Sacrament, you can see Jesus, the Son of Mary,
each day.

> *Do this now*: Ask our Lady to give you the eyes of faith to
> see Jesus in the Mass, in the Consecration and in Holy
> Communion, and in His Eucharistic Presence in the tab-
> ernacle or monstrance. Pray, "Mary, give me the eyes to
> see Jesus in His Eucharistic Presence and to love and adore
> Him with your Immaculate Heart!"

Our Lady of Sorrows

As the prophet Simeon marvels at the Infant Jesus, he foretells a sorrow that will penetrate Mary's Immaculate Heart: "Behold, this child is set for the fall and rising of many in Israel, and for a sign that is spoken against (and a sword will pierce through your own soul also), that thoughts out of many hearts may be revealed" (Luke 2:34–35). Mary does not flinch, nor does she bewail her fate. She is open to the will of God in absolutely everything, including all the sufferings that God in His divine providence intends to send her.

Do this now: Resolve, like the Blessed Mother, to accept graciously all the misfortunes and sufferings that our Lord permits you to face. Resolve to bear them peacefully and without anger or resentment and to use each one as an occasion for you to renew your consecration to our Lord through His Mother. For her many spiritual sufferings the great Saint Alphonsus Liguori called Mary the Queen of Martyrs.

Your Sorrows

When a child falls down and scrapes his knee, his mother runs to his aid, lifts him up, and kisses and bandages the wound. Whenever you fall, our Lady is always ready to pick you up out of the mud, clean you up, change your clothes, and help you start again with renewed hope.

Do this now: Turn to our Lady in good times and in bad—and not only when bad things happen to you but also when you do bad things. Never be afraid to open up and pour out from the depths of your broken heart your deep sorrows, your wounds, your bruises, and even your scars.

TOTAL CONSECRATION

---

*Finally, prepare to consecrate
yourself to Jesus through our Lady*

As you move forward on your journey to total consecration,
travel to Jerusalem with Saint Joseph and Mary with Jesus in
her arms. Relive the encounter with the elderly prophet Simeon.
Meditate on the prophetic message about Jesus' death and our
Lady's collaboration in His suffering. Share in the suffering of
Jesus and Mary, but also talk to our Lady about your own crosses
and sufferings. Consecration to our Lady means giving her all we
have and are. This includes our struggles, our sufferings, and even
our failures. She is always there, ready and willing to stretch out
her loving hands to lift us up and to clasp us to her Immaculate
Heart!

Day 5: Fifth Joyful Mystery

THE FINDING OF THE CHILD JESUS IN THE TEMPLE

Luke 2:41–52
Read slowly and prayerfully

Now his parents went to Jerusalem every year at the feast of the Passover. And when he was twelve years old, they went up according to custom; and when the feast was ended, as they were returning, the boy Jesus stayed behind in Jerusalem. His parents did not know it, but supposing him to be in the company they went a day's journey, and they sought him among their kinsfolk and acquaintances; and when they did not find him, they returned to Jerusalem, seeking him. After three days they found him in the Temple, sitting among the teachers, listening to them and asking them questions; and all who heard him were amazed at his understanding and his answers. And when they saw him they were astonished; and his mother said to him, "Son, why have you treated us so? Behold, your father and I have been looking for you anxiously." And he said to them, "How is it that you sought me? Did you not know that I must be in my Father's house?" And they did not understand the saying which he spoke to them. And he went down with them and came to Nazareth, and was obedient to them; and his mother kept all these things in her heart.

And Jesus increased in wisdom and in stature, and in favor with God and man.

Meditate on Jesus lost in Jerusalem

Our Lady and Saint Joseph search sorrowfully for Jesus for three days. These must have been among the most painful days in their lives. How could this have happened? When they finally find Jesus and Mary tells Him of her sorrow in losing Him for three days, He responds "How is it that you sought me? Did you not know that I must be in my Father's house?"—an answer that puzzles her and Joseph.

When similar painful, puzzling things happen to you, you can receive extraordinary consolation by sharing them with our Lady. You can speak to her as a little child would speak to his mother. Indeed, although Mary is the Mother of God and the Mother of the Church, she is also and always your Mother. Remember what Our Lady of Guadalupe told Saint Juan Diego when she appeared to him: "Do not be afraid. Am I not your Mother? You are in the crossing of my arms; you are in my shadow; you are in my apron (*tilma*), the covering over my womb."

Consider thoughtfully

From Sin to Grace
If you have had the misfortune of losing Jesus in the depths of your heart due to a mortal sin, never despair! Return to Jesus

through prayer, penance, the sacrament of Confession, and total trust in Jesus' infinite mercy!

Do this now: Pray now and often throughout your day, "Jesus, Son of Mary, I trust in You!"

The Search for Jesus

Saint Joseph and our Lady searched for Jesus for three long days.

Do this now: In imitation of Mary, seek constantly for ways to find Jesus in your life and to draw closer to Him. Strive to love Him fervently and to follow Him closely. True joy and happiness, our Lady teaches us, is in knowing, loving and serving Jesus, our Lord, God, and Savior.

How Did She Lose Him?

How Mary lost her beloved Child for three days is a mystery that neither she nor Joseph could explain. How many times does God visit us with similar mysteries and sometimes very painful ones that don't seem to make any sense whatsoever? Some of them may have been so upsetting that they've even led you to question God's providential design in your life.

Do this now: When life's events baffle and distress you, turn to our Lady. Talk freely and intimately with her about them. She is the best of listeners, never in a hurry, and she understands your heart better than you understand it yourself. Even though these mysteries may not have easy solutions, sharing them with our Lady can be an extraordinary consolation! Open up your heart now and speak to our Lady.

Where They Find Jesus

They find Jesus in the Temple of Jerusalem, standing in the midst of the doctors of the Law, listening to them and asking them questions. Remember that Jesus is only twelve years old! Never have these doctors of the Law met anyone as young and brilliant as this boy!

Do this now: With the doctors of the Law, acknowledge Jesus as your best teacher and resolve to turn to Him in prayer in those times when life baffles you or you can't find your way. Listen to Him patiently, and you may soon hear Him speak, showing you the true way, as He showed it to the doctors of the Law.

Jesus' Obedience and Growth

A rebellious, proud, and disobedient spirit is repugnant to God, whereas a humble, docile spirit pleases Him. Although Jesus was Himself God, He chose to be humble and docile, even toward creatures He brought into being. Says the evangelist: "And he ... was obedient to them; and ... [he] increased in wisdom and in stature, and in favor with God and man."

Do this now: Turn to our Lady and beg her for the grace to be as obedient to God as Jesus was to Mary and Saint Joseph. Ask her to help you obey the Word of God, the Catholic Church, the Ten Commandments, a well-formed conscience, and the inspirations of the Holy Spirit.

Our Lady of Wisdom

One of the many mystical and poetic titles for our Lady is "Seat of Wisdom." Wisdom is the greatest of the gifts of the Holy Spirit, and it leads us to relish the things of God. Remember the words of Jesus: "Seek first his kingdom and his righteousness, and all these things shall be yours as well" (Matt. 6:33).

Do this now: Ask our Lady for an ever deeper and dynamic gift of wisdom in your heart and in your life!

Finally, sit at the feet of Jesus

Just as Mary suffered when Jesus was lost, so have you suffered from losses. Perhaps you are wounded by physical pain and sufferings, disease, the death of a loved one, or the loss of your job. Maybe you or someone you love is struggling with drugs, alcohol, or a loss of faith. Perhaps you've lost your spouse through death or unfaithfulness and a painful separation. Do not keep these sorrows to yourself, but bring them to our Lady. Indeed, an integral part of your consecration to our Lady is trust in her and your willingness to tell her all that is going on in your life—even the most painful difficulties you've been hiding for many years!

Once you do so, you will, like Jesus, grow in wisdom, knowledge, and grace before God and man! You will find yourself regularly sitting spiritually at the feet of Jesus, your Teacher, fervently imploring Him, "Speak, Jesus, Son of Mary. Speak: your servant is listening!"

FIRST AND SECOND REPETITIONS

On days 6 and 7 repeat one of the mysteries on which you meditated this week. You might choose a meditation during which God moved you and poured abundant consolations into your soul. There may be more consolations waiting for you. Like a bee that returns to a flower for more nectar, return to the flower of this meditation for more spiritual nectar.

St. Ignatius suggests that sometimes it's good to choose a meditation during which you experienced desolation. Why? Desolation in prayer often manifests a certain resistance on our part to grace. Ask the Holy Spirit to help you break down that resistance through repetition.

Enter into the meditation, beginning with the steps found on the inside of the front cover.

Week 2

THE LUMINOUS MYSTERIES

Day 1: First Luminous Mystery

THE BAPTISM OF JESUS

Matthew 3:13–17
Read slowly and prayerfully

Then Jesus came from Galilee to the Jordan to John, to be baptized by him. John would have prevented him, saying, "I need to be baptized by you, and do you come to me?" But Jesus answered him, "Let it be so now; for thus it is fitting for us to fulfil all righteousness." Then he consented. And when Jesus was baptized, he went up immediately from the water, and behold, the heavens were opened and he saw the Spirit of God descending like a dove, and alighting on him; and lo, a voice from heaven, saying, "This is my beloved Son, with whom I am well pleased."

John 3:1–6
Read slowly and prayerfully

Now there was a man of the Pharisees, named Nicodemus, a ruler of the Jews. This man came to Jesus by night and said to him, "Rabbi, we know that you are a teacher come from God; for no one can do these signs that you do, unless God is with him." Jesus answered him, "Truly, truly, I say to you, unless one is born anew, he cannot see the kingdom of God." Nicodemus said to him, "How can a man be born when he is old? Can he enter a second time into his mother's womb and be born?" Jesus answered, "Truly, truly, I say to you, unless one is born of water and the Spirit, he cannot enter the kingdom of God. That which is born of the flesh is flesh, and that which is born of the Spirit is spirit.

Meditate on the Baptism of Jesus

Jesus' humanity was given to Him by His Mother, Mary, and it started at the moment of the Annunciation when our Lady said yes to God: "And the Word became flesh and dwelt among us" (John 1:14). As you prepare yourself for consecration to Jesus through Mary, contemplate the Luminous Mysteries of the Rosary, also known as the Mysteries of Light, given to us by our late pope Saint John Paul II.

The Luminous Mysteries, focusing on the public life of our Lord, are especially pertinent since Mary is rightly known as *Stella Maris* (Star of the Sea) and *Stella Matutina* (Star of the Morning). She can obtain for you ever increasing light in your mind, in your heart, and in your soul!

The first Luminous Mystery is the Baptism of Jesus. When He descends into the waters of the Jordan River and is baptized, there is a Trinitarian manifestation of the Father, the Son, and the Holy Spirit: the voice of the Father is heard declaring that He is well pleased with His Son; the Son, Jesus, has descended into the waters of the Jordan, thereby sanctifying them; and the Holy Spirit, in the form of a dove, descends on Jesus.

Consider thoughtfully

Jesus Embarks on His Public Life

When the time comes for Jesus to leave His home in Nazareth, as designated by the Father, He goes first to the Jordan River to be baptized by His cousin, Saint John the Baptist. Jesus takes leave of His Mother, hugging her goodbye with great tenderness and devotion as He heads off toward His mission and His destiny — the salvation of the world.

Do this now: Be with Mary as her eyes and heart follow Jesus heading toward the Jordan. Her eyes are fixed on Him until He disappears in the distance. Like Mary, strive always to keep your eyes and your heart fixed on Jesus at all times. Speak to Mary about the departure of Jesus, and share the sentiments in her Immaculate Heart.

Jesus' Baptism and Yours

Beseech our Lady to help you gain a richer understanding of your Baptism, of how it unites you to God, and of the enormous responsibilities entailed by this first of the sacraments. Remember that it was at Jesus' Baptism in the Jordan that the Holy Trinity — Three Persons in one God — was first made known to us.

Do this now: Renew your baptismal commitment through fervent prayer to Mary, asking her to deepen your union with the Father, the Son, and the Holy Spirit.

Original Sin

Our Lady was conceived without Original Sin. Through your Baptism you were freed from the stain of Original Sin. Mary can help you through the graces of your Baptism to avoid temptations and to refrain from sin.

Do this now: Resolve to say often, in times of temptation and even at other times, the prayer on the Miraculous Medal: "O Mary, conceived without sin, pray for us who have recourse to thee!"

Mary Will Crush the Devil's Head

Before you were baptized, the priest prayed for your liberation from the Devil. Remember that Genesis warns the Devil about his battle with Mary and Jesus: "I will put enmity between you and the woman, and between your seed and her seed; he shall bruise your head, and you shall bruise his heel" (Gen. 3:15).

Do this now: Mary is a powerful foe of the Devil. Ask her to help you reject the Devil's seductions, and resolve to call on her for help whenever you face temptation.

You Are a Temple of the Holy Spirit

Through Baptism you enter into an intimate relationship with the Holy Spirit and become His living temple. Our Lady can draw you deeper into that union, for she is not only the Holy Spirit's temple but also His Mystical Spouse.

Do this now: So much does God love Mary that, in the words of Saint Louis de Montfort, "The Holy Spirit flings Himself into the souls of those who love Mary." Implore our Lady to help you prepare a resting place for the Holy Spirit in your heart.

You Are a Child of God

Our Lady is the chosen Daughter of God the Father. Through Baptism you also become a son or daughter of God—what great dignity!

Do this now: If you have fallen short of this dignity, our Lady can help you to get up and resume your efforts to live up to the heights of your calling! Ask her for help now!

You Are a Brother or Sister of Jesus

From the Cross, our Lord gave you Mary to be your Mother (see John 19:27). Through Baptism you became a brother or sister of Jesus. Mary is your Mother and Jesus is your Brother — what joy and consolation!

Do this now: Mary can help you to comprehend your membership in the Family of God. Ask her to pray that your relationship with Jesus — your Brother — will grow continually until you are united with Him forever in Heaven.

Finally, renew your baptismal commitment

Take a moment right now to renew your resolve to live to the maximum the vocational call and responsibilities of your Baptism. Ask our Lady to help you to avoid sin or to be repentant of your sins and to pursue holiness. Implore her to help you to reject the tactics of the Devil — our chief enemy on the way to salvation. In this way, through the prayers and intercession of Mary, you will become what you are called to be: holy.

Day 2: Second Luminous Mystery

JESUS AND MARY AT THE WEDDING FEAST AT CANA

John 2:1–12
Read slowly and prayerfully

On the third day there was a marriage at Cana in Galilee, and the mother of Jesus was there; Jesus also was invited to the marriage, with his disciples. When the wine failed, the mother of Jesus said to him, "They have no wine." And Jesus said to her, "O woman, what have you to do with me? My hour has not yet come." His mother said to the servants, "Do whatever he tells you." Now six stone jars were standing there, for the Jewish rites of purification, each holding twenty or thirty gallons. Jesus said to them, "Fill the jars with water." And they filled them up to the brim. He said to them, "Now draw some out, and take it to the steward of the feast." So they took it. When the steward of the feast tasted the water now become wine, and did not know where it came from (though the servants who had drawn the water knew), the steward of the feast called the bridegroom and said to him, "Every man serves the good wine first; and when men have drunk freely, then the poor wine; but you have kept the good wine until now." This, the first of his signs, Jesus did at Cana in Galilee, and manifested his glory; and his disciples believed in him.

After this he went down to Capernaum, with his mother and his brethren and his disciples; and there they stayed for a few days.

Meditate on the Wedding at Cana

Soon after His baptism, Jesus attends a wedding along with some of His followers and his loving Mother, Mary. There, through the intercession of our Lady, Jesus performs His first public miracle.

As Saint Ignatius of Loyola teaches about contemplation, you should strive with the help of God's grace to enter into this scene, to see in your imagination the persons, their words and their actions and derive much fruit from this Spiritual Exercise with Our Lady present there with Jesus.

Consider thoughtfully

The Characters of Mary and Jesus

Jesus is attractive. He is manly and strong; at the same time He is meek and humble. He has extraordinary poise and inspires great confidence. He invites you to enter into conversation with Him. And Mary? As Saint Louis de Montfort reminds us, she is the masterpiece of creation. The beauty of her soul radiates from her countenance. Modesty, purity, humility, joy, and poise all decorate her exterior comportment.

Do this now: Picture Mary and Jesus sitting side by side at the banquet table. Imagine that you are seated with them. They are happy to have you as a fellow guest. They enjoy your company; they want to enter into deep friendship with you. Speak to them.

Your Own Worries

Mary and Jesus look into your eyes and see that there's something heavy on your heart; there's a problem weighing you down; it's heavy on your heart and on your whole being! Jesus invites you: "Come to me, all who labor and are heavy laden, and I will give you rest. Take my yoke upon you, and learn from me; for I am gentle and lowly in heart, and you will find rest for your souls. For my yoke is easy, and my burden is light" (Matt. 11:28–30).

Do this now: If wounds are not treated, they get worse; they fester and can get seriously infected. Tell Mary about your past wounds and even your present ones. She is known as "Health of the Sick" and can help heal you.

There Is No More Wine

With her attentive eye, our Lady perceives a serious problem — there is no longer enough wine for the feast. That will embarrass the wedding couple. Mary informs Jesus of the problem. As a result of her intercession, He transforms water into wine — wine of the best quality.

Do this now: Learn from this incident the central role that Mary plays in our lives. It is she who notices the need for more wine, and it is her intercession that leads Jesus to perform His first miracle. Go to Mary now, and ask her to implore Jesus to perform in your life the miracles—large and small—that are necessary for your growth in faith and love, and for your upcoming consecration to Jesus.

Your Own Water and Wine

As is usually the case with events in the lives of Jesus and Mary, the miracle at Cana has a symbolic as well as a literal meaning. In this case, we can understand the water to be symbolic of our shortcomings, our defects, and our moral failures—in a word, our sinfulness.

Do this now: Bring to Mary the sin that has been dragging you down, tainting your spiritual life, demeaning and degrading your dignity as a son or daughter of God. Is it impatience? Impurity? Anger? Gluttony? Envy or jealousy? Greed or materialism? Sloth? Beg our Lady, through her powerful intercession, to change your water into splendid, exquisite wine.

Finally, continue speaking to Jesus and Mary

Your consecration is very much related to open, trusting confidence in talking to Mary as you have just done spiritually at the Wedding Feast at Cana. May this wonderful conversation that you had with Mary and Jesus carry on all the rest of your life.

Day 3: Third Luminous Mystery

THE PROCLAMATION OF THE KINGDOM OF GOD AND THE CALL TO CONVERSION

Matthew 5:1–12
Read slowly and prayerfully

Seeing the crowds, he went up on the mountain, and when he sat down his disciples came to him. And he opened his mouth and taught them, saying:

"Blessed are the poor in spirit, for theirs is the kingdom of heaven.

"Blessed are those who mourn, for they shall be comforted.

"Blessed are the meek, for they shall inherit the earth.

"Blessed are those who hunger and thirst for righteousness, for they shall be satisfied.

"Blessed are the merciful, for they shall obtain mercy.

"Blessed are the pure in heart, for they shall see God.

"Blessed are the peacemakers, for they shall be called sons of God.

"Blessed are those who are persecuted for righteousness' sake, for theirs is the kingdom of heaven.

"Blessed are you when men revile you and persecute you and utter all kinds of evil against you falsely on my account. Rejoice and be glad, for your reward is great in heaven, for so men persecuted the prophets who were before you."

Matthew 7:7–11
Read slowly and prayerfully

Ask, and it will be given you; seek, and you will find; knock, and it will be opened to you. For every one who asks receives, and he who seeks finds, and to him who knocks it will be opened. Or what man of you, if his son asks him for bread, will give him a stone? Or if he asks for a fish, will give him a serpent? If you then, who are evil, know how to give good gifts to your children, how much more will your Father who is in heaven give good things to those who ask him!

Meditate on the Proclamation of the
Kingdom of God and the Call to Conversion

The very first words of Jesus in His public ministry were a call to conversion: "Repent, for the kingdom of heaven is at hand" (Matt. 4:17). It is a call that each of us must answer, for we must all humbly admit that we are sinners and are therefore spiritually sick. Saint John Paul II called Marian sanctuaries "spiritual clinics" where sinners go to be healed. We can all go to our Lady for healing. As we follow Jesus in His preaching, especially when He speaks of conversion, and as we follow our Lady, the first and greatest disciple of Jesus, we become aware of what they both long for most: the salvation of souls, each and every one, including yours.

Consider thoughtfully

Mary Leads Us to Jesus

Mary is not a detour away from Jesus. On the contrary, she is a solid, firm bridge that unites us with Jesus. Not only was she the first and best disciple of Jesus and a true listener to the Word of God; she also put into practice the Word of God. We are to "be doers of the word, and not hearers only" (James 1:22).

Do this now: In imitation of Mary, ask for the grace to listen attentively to Jesus and to put into practice His words. "Not every one who says to me, 'Lord, Lord,' shall enter the kingdom of heaven, but he who does the will of my Father who is in heaven" (Matt. 7:21). Beseech our Lady to help you become be a true and faithful follower of Jesus. Your prayer will definitely be heard. Recall that Saint Louis de Montfort tells us that Mary is the quickest, shortest, and the easiest path to Jesus.

Listen to Our Lady

The last words of our Lady recorded in the Bible are: "Do whatever He tells you" (John 2:5). This is the best advice we can possibly imagine. If we would simply put into practice these words of Mary, we would be filled with peace and joy, and we would be on the sure path to salvation, or, if you like, the highway to heaven!

Do this now: Entreat our Lady to help you come to know more precisely what Jesus is telling you today—and resolve to ask this every day. Ask, as well, for the strength to do whatever He tells you.

Remember That Jesus Heals

Jesus came into this world to heal us as well as to save us. As the prophet says: "With his stripes we are healed" (Isa. 53:5). Jesus healed the blind, the deaf, the mute, paralytics, and lepers, and He even raised some from the dead. He came to heal the afflicted.

Do this now: Beseech our Lady for the grace of a daily conversion of heart, for the love of Jesus. Implore her to help you see your major weak points, and beg for her intercession in your efforts to conquer them! If you are suffering in soul or body, ask Jesus to heal you as He has healed so many others over the ages. If possible, visit a Marian shrine near you so that you may pray there with thousands of others who ask Jesus, through Mary, to grant them healing.

Conversion and Confession

Our Lady, the Mother of Mercy and Refuge of Sinners, constantly prays for your conversion, your growth in holiness, and your perseverance in grace. Your spiritual transformation can come about in many ways, but the most efficacious means are the sacraments, especially the sacrament of Confession.

Do this now: Resolve to go to Confession at the next available opportunity, and to frequent Confession regularly thereafter. Ask our Lady, Mother of Mercy and Refuge of Sinners, to help you to make better confessions. They will bring healing to your soul and help you to pray regularly for the conversion of others who are in need of prayer. Also, ask our Lady for the grace to bring others to this source of healing, mercy, and conversion.

Fatima and Lourdes

At Lourdes, France, our Lady encouraged Saint Bernadette to practice penance for the conversion of sinners. Years later, at Fatima, Portugal, our Lady encouraged three other children to do penance and offer up sacrifices for the conversion of poor sinners. So important are sacrifices and penance that our Lady said very sadly that many souls are lost for the simple reason that not enough people offer prayers and sacrifices for them.

Do this now: Our Lady wants you to collaborate with her in loving Jesus by praying, working, and sacrificing for the salvation of immortal souls. She is looking lovingly at you now and asking you: "What can you give, do, offer, or sacrifice of what you have and who you are so as to obtain the conversion of poor sinners?" Implore our Lady to help you work with her for the conversion of sinners by offering up small sacrifices to her Heart and to the Heart of Jesus for the conversion of sinners.

Pray for Others

In the sanctuaries of our Lady, and through her powerful intercession, miracles happen constantly: healings and conversions. Souls that have been away from the Church for years, even decades, return. Through our Lady's most powerful prayers of intercession, the most hardened sinners often receive the grace to renounce their sinful lives and turn fully to the love and mercy of the Sacred Heart of Jesus — the Heart that was formed in Mary's immaculate womb for nine months. Mary's prayers can bring the most serious sinner to tears of conversion and a change of life!

Do this now: Speak to our Lady about the conversion of sinners and Jesus' call to conversion: "Repent, for the kingdom of heaven is at hand" (Matt. 4:17). Ask her for the grace to understand with greater depth the value of one immortal soul so that you will be motivated to pray harder for the conversion of sinners, redeemed by Jesus' Precious Blood, which was given to Him through Mary.

Finally, imitate their great love

To love Jesus and Mary truly, you must come to desire what they desire. In Saint Faustina Kowalska's *Diary of Divine Mercy in My Soul*, Jesus said that the best way to measure true love is the willingness to suffer for the one you love. Entreat our Lady that you may come to have such love, for it can be a powerful tool in her hands to help in the conversion of immortal souls.

Day 4: Fourth Luminous Mystery

THE TRANSFIGURATION OF JESUS

Matthew 17:1–13
Read slowly and prayerfully

And after six days Jesus took with him Peter and James and John his brother, and led them up a high mountain apart. And he was transfigured before them, and his face shone like the sun, and his garments became white as light. And behold, there appeared to them Moses and Elijah, talking with him. And Peter said to Jesus, "Lord, it is well that we are here; if you wish, I will make three booths here, one for you and one for Moses and one for Elijah."

He was still speaking, when lo, a bright cloud overshadowed them, and a voice from the cloud said, "This is my beloved Son, with whom I am well pleased; listen to him." When the disciples heard this, they fell on their faces, and were filled with awe. But Jesus came and touched them, saying, "Rise, and have no fear." And when they lifted up their eyes, they saw no one but Jesus only.

And as they were coming down the mountain, Jesus commanded them, "Tell no one the vision, until the Son of man is raised from the dead." And the disciples asked him, "Then why do the scribes say that first Elijah must come?" He replied, "Elijah does come, and he is to restore all things; but I tell you that Elijah has already come, and they did not know him, but did to him whatever they pleased. So also the Son of man will suffer at their hands." Then the disciples understood that he was speaking to them of John the Baptist.

Meditate on the Transfiguration

As you consider attentively these biblical passages on the Transfiguration, ask the Holy Spirit to speak to you in a special way. In this moment, and in all the days of preparation for your consecration, be docile, open, and willing to listen to the Word of God. Our Lady pondered and meditated deeply upon the Word of God. Ask her to help you to do the same!

Consider thoughtfully

The Formation of Jesus' Body

It was Mary most holy who formed the Sacred Body of Jesus in her womb, giving to Him from her own body His blood, veins, arteries, eyes, lungs, and even His most Sacred Heart.

Do this now: Ask our Lady, through her most powerful prayers, to intercede for you so that your heart may be purified, formed, and re-created to be more and more like the Sacred Heart of Jesus. As a result of her intercession, may you be able to say with Saint Paul, "It is no longer I who live, but Christ who lives in me" (Gal. 2:20).

Friendship with Jesus

One of the images we see in the Transfiguration of Jesus is that of human friendship. Jesus ardently desired to enter into deep friendship with those men He chose—especially Peter, James, and John. These were the three who accompanied Him as He ascended the Mount of the Transfiguration. At the Last Supper Jesus will call them "friends."

> *Do this now*: Jesus walked with and talked to His friends. He wants to walk with and talk to you right now. Jesus wants to enter into a very deep friendship with you right now. Spend some time talking to Him as a friend.

Mary Knew Jesus Best of All

No greater intimacy exists in this world, on a human level, than between a baby and his mother as he is formed in the womb. After He was born, Jesus spent most of His life on earth with Saint Joseph and Mary in their home in Nazareth. Mary watched Jesus, talked to Him, listened to Him, contemplated His face and His eyes—for thirty years. Nobody on earth, or even in heaven, aside from God Himself, ever had a deeper friendship with Jesus than His Mother, Mary most holy.

> *Do this now*: Ask Mary to help you to enter into deeper friendship with Jesus. Talk to her with total confidence. She is your Mother, and you are her beloved child.

Our Lady of the Way

There is a very well known song in both Italian and Spanish called "Santa Maria del Camino"—Our Lady of the Way. As Jesus climbed the Mount of the Transfiguration, His Apostles walked with Him, side by side. You can likewise have our Lady by your side.

Do this now: In your travels in life, ask our Lady to accompany you and never to abandon you. She will always point you to Jesus and will help you to climb with Him and enter into deep union with Him.

Your Calvary and Mary

Jesus' climbing calls to mind your own ascent, your personal Calvary. Never presume that you have the strength to carry your cross by yourself. Our Lady will help you every step of the way.

Do this now: Life without Jesus and Mary can be very sad, depressing, and even bitter. That's why you should be eager to cry out to Mary in prayer: "Hail, holy Queen, Mother of mercy, hail, our life, our sweetness, and our hope. To thee do we cry, poor banished children of Eve: to thee do we send up our sighs, mourning, and weeping in this valley of tears. Turn then, most gracious Advocate, thine eyes of mercy toward us, and after this our exile, show unto us the blessed fruit of thy womb, Jesus, O merciful, O loving, O sweet Virgin Mary! Amen."

We Are All Pilgrims

We are all pilgrims heading toward our eternal destiny — which is heaven. As we climb the mountain toward heaven, Mary can guide us, help us, encourage us, and comfort us.

Do this now: Spend time talking to Mary about your past journey in life, your present journey, and even your future journey — for your whole life should be a pilgrimage, assisted by the love of Jesus and Mary.

Our Lady, Star of the Sea
The great Marian Doctor Saint Bernard offers the following: A ship at sea is being assaulted by constant waves. The wind beats mercilessly against its rudder. The waters are starting to enter in — there is a real danger of the ship's capsizing and sinking. Suddenly a beautiful star breaks through the night clouds and glimmers forth. This star seems to be pointing toward the shore. The captain, with great confidence, looks long at the star and decides to follow it. The waves subside, the winds abate, the storm fades away. With almost unspeakable peace and swiftness the ship arrives safely at the shore. The ship, the captain, and all the members are saved, thanks to the Star of the Sea.

Do this now: Resolve to lift your gaze to Our Lady, Star of the Sea, in the midst of the storms, afflictions, trials, and temptations in your life. She will safely direct you to the port of salvation, to your eternal home, which is heaven.

The Mountaintop and the Shore
Both the top of the Mount of the Transfiguration and the shore symbolize heavenly rest at the end of the journey, by land or by sea. Jesus wants you to arrive there by the straightest path, and He yearns to walk with you, to talk with you, and to accompany you the whole way. Our Lady also wants to keep you close to her on this perilous journey. But it's easy to give up because the mountain is high and the path challenging; and it's easy to sink in the waves of sensuality and selfishness and give up the fight.

Do this now: The devil has a deadly fear of Mary and even of her Holy Name, because she always leads souls to Jesus. In moments of temptation, don't continue to journey alone: resolve to call upon the Holy Names of Jesus and Mary.

Finally, turn to Mary throughout your journey through life

Saint Ignatius of Loyola was particularly devoted to *La Madonna de la Strada*—literally translated as "Our Lady of the Street" but loosely translated as "Our Lady of the Way." As you make your way through life, call out to Our Lady of the Way. As you climb your mountains and make your sea journeys, spend some moments talking to Mary, opening your heart to its very depths. Tell her all that is going on right now in your life. Ask her to be with you always, every step along the way until you reach heaven. Remember that the quickest path to the Sacred Heart of Jesus is through the Immaculate Heart of Mary!

Day 5: Fifth Luminous Mystery

THE INSTITUTION OF
THE HOLY EUCHARIST

Matthew 26:26–28
Read slowly and prayerfully

Now as they were eating, Jesus took bread, and blessed, and broke it, and gave it to the disciples and said, "Take, eat; this is my body." And he took a cup, and when he had given thanks he gave it to them, saying, "Drink of it, all of you; for this is my blood of the covenant, which is poured out for many for the forgiveness of sins.

John 6:47–59
Read slowly and prayerfully

"Truly, truly, I say to you, he who believes has eternal life. I am the bread of life. Your fathers ate the manna in the wilderness, and they died. This is the bread which comes down from heaven, that a man may eat of it and not die. I am the living bread which came down from heaven; if any one eats of this bread, he will live forever; and the bread which I shall give for the life of the world is my flesh."

The Jews then disputed among themselves, saying, "How can this man give us his flesh to eat?" So Jesus said to them, "Truly, truly, I say to you, unless you eat the flesh of the Son of man and drink his blood, you have no life in you; he who eats my flesh and drinks my blood has eternal life, and I will raise him up at the last day. For my flesh is food indeed, and my blood is drink indeed. He who eats my flesh and drinks my blood abides in me, and I in him. As the living Father sent me, and I live because of the Father, so he who eats me will live because of me. This is the bread which came down from heaven, not such as the fathers ate and died; he who eats this bread will live forever." This he said in the synagogue, as he taught at Capernaum.

Meditate on the Eucharist

Two of the greatest gifts that our Lord and Savior Jesus Christ left for us as the most powerful means to get to our eternal goal — heaven — were the Holy Eucharist and the Blessed Virgin Mary. Jesus left us the great gift of the Holy Eucharist at the Last Supper on Holy Thursday, which was the first Holy Mass.

Consider thoughtfully

Our Lady and the Eucharist
Mary always connects us with her Son. She nourished within her most pure body, in her precious womb, the Body and Blood

of Jesus. Every time you receive Holy Communion, you receive that same Body and Blood, originally given to us by Mary. Meditation on this fact will bring you greater appreciation for the Holy Sacrifice of the Mass, the most Holy Eucharist, and your reception of Holy Communion.

Do this now: Ask Mary for greater faith in, love for, and devotion to the Holy Eucharist. Implore her for an ardent desire to receive her Son in Holy Communion more frequently and more fervently.

Our Lady of Guadalupe, Mexico

The three most famous Marian apparitions—Guadalupe, Lourdes, and Fatima—each had a very strong Eucharistic thrust. The first occurred in 1531. Our Lady appeared in Guadalupe to the peasant Juan Diego and asked that a church be built there on Tepeyac Hill. Why a church? So that Holy Mass would be celebrated there and the people could receive Jesus, the Son of Mary, in Holy Communion. Now millions of pilgrims come every year to visit our Lady and to receive Jesus in Holy Communion.

Do this now: As Mary's womb once contained Jesus, the tabernacle in your church is the house of Jesus now. The tabernacle is the living heart of the Church. Mary, who helped form the Sacred Heart of Jesus in her womb for nine months, helped form the living heart of the Church at the foot of the Cross—for the Church was born from the blood and water flowing from the pierced Heart of Jesus Crucified. As you attend Mass in preparation for your consecration, ask Mary to help your spiritual heart beat in unison with the Sacred Heart of Jesus in the tabernacle. Strive to awaken in yourself greater reverence for the Eucharist and greater devotion to it.

Our Lady of Lourdes, France

At Lourdes, our Lady appeared eighteen times to a simple, humble, frail little girl, Bernadette Soubirous. Our Lady asked that a church be built there. Many miracles have occurred in Lourdes, most of them at dusk during the Eucharistic procession outside the church. The same Jesus, the Son of Mary, who healed so many people of their sicknesses is still healing people today when they entrust themselves to Him and Mary.

Do this now: Beg our Lady, Health of the Sick, through her prayers to Jesus, for the healing of your whole person, for the healing of memories that come back to torture you, and for your soul, wounded by past sins. Ask her to help you break bad habits that enslave you and to heal your body, which may have been used more to sin and to offend God than to glorify His Holy Name! Healing comes powerfully through our Lady's prayers, which lead us to Jesus present in His Church, His Mystical Body. But most especially healing comes through Confession and the worthy reception of Holy Communion.

Our Lady of Fatima, Portugal

At Fatima, our Lady appeared six times to three young shepherds—Jacinta and Francisco Marto and their cousin Lucia de los Santos. Before our Lady appeared to the children, the angel of Portugal appeared. Strikingly, the final appearance of the angel was marked with a Eucharistic miracle that changed their lives. Suspended in the air above the angel was a chalice that contained the Precious Blood of Jesus; below the chalice was a large Host. The angel told the children to receive the Body and Blood of Jesus that was so often offended. In other words, the angel wanted them to make a Communion of reparation for sins against the Holy Eucharist. This they did. Jacinta and Francisco received from the chalice—a prophecy of their early deaths. Lucia received the Sacred Host. Our Lady asked that a church be built there. Why a church? Once again the response was the same: to honor, love, and adore Jesus—the Son of Mary—who descends from heaven in the hands of the priest in every Consecration, and then descends into human hearts every time they receive Him in Holy Communion.

Do this now: Mary formed the mind of Jesus within her womb for nine months. We have the mind of Christ when we receive Holy Communion worthily. Beseech our Lady, as well as Blessed Jacinta and Blessed Francisco, for the grace to receive Jesus with great love, devotion, fervor, and frequency in Holy Communion!

Finally, hunger to receive the Bread of Life often

To love Mary is to love Jesus, and to love Jesus is to love His Mystical Body, which is the Catholic Church. When you love Jesus, you have a burning desire to receive Him in your heart, your mind, and your soul in Holy Communion! Saint John Paul II said that Mary's yes (*fiat*) at the Annunciation is akin to our "Amen" before receiving Holy Communion. The result is the same: we receive the real presence of Jesus. Ask our Lady for a greater hunger and thirst to receive Jesus, the Bread of Life.

Days 6 and 7

FIRST AND SECOND REPETITIONS

On days 6 and 7 repeat one of the mysteries on which you meditated this week. You might choose a meditation during which God moved you and poured abundant consolations into your soul. There may be more consolations waiting for you. Like a bee that returns to a flower for more nectar, return to the flower of this meditation for more spiritual nectar.

St. Ignatius suggests that sometimes it's good to choose a meditation during which you experienced desolation. Why? Desolation in prayer often manifests a certain resistance on our part to grace. Ask the Holy Spirit to help you break down that resistance through repetition.

Enter into the meditation, beginning with the steps found on pages 10 and 11.

Week 3

The Sorrowful Mysteries

Day 1: First Sorrowful Mystery

THE AGONY OF JESUS IN THE GARDEN OF GETHSEMANE

Matthew 26:36–46
Read slowly and prayerfully

Then Jesus went with them to a place called Gethsemane, and he said to his disciples, "Sit here, while I go yonder and pray." And taking with him Peter and the two sons of Zebedee, he began to be sorrowful and troubled. Then he said to them, "My soul is very sorrowful, even to death; remain here, and watch with me." And going a little farther he fell on his face and prayed, "My Father, if it be possible, let this cup pass from me; nevertheless, not as I will, but as thou wilt." And he came to the disciples and found them sleeping; and he said to Peter, "So, could you not watch with me one hour? Watch and pray that you may not enter into temptation; the spirit indeed is willing, but the flesh is weak." Again, for the second time, he went away and prayed, "My Father, if this cannot pass unless I drink it, thy will be done." And again he came and found them sleeping, for their eyes were heavy. So, leaving them again, he went away and prayed for the third time, saying the same words. Then he came to the disciples and said to them, "Are you still sleeping and taking your rest? Behold, the hour is at hand, and the Son of man is betrayed into the hands of sinners. Rise, let us be going; see, my betrayer is at hand."

Meditate on Jesus in Gethsemane

Adam and Eve committed the Original Sin in a garden. To atone for the sins of Adam and Eve and the sins of all humanity, Jesus suffers intensely in another garden. The darkness in Gethsemane recalls the darkness of sin that surrounds Jesus, a darkness that Judas has now entered.

Consider thoughtfully

Jesus and His Weak Friends

Jesus takes into Gethsemane three of his faithful friends—Peter, James, and John—hoping that their compassion will help Him bear the suffering He is about to undergo. His friends, however, fail Him by falling asleep.

> *Do this now:* Recall the many times you have fallen asleep while praying, or worse yet, have failed to get out of bed to pray when Jesus invited you to communion with Him in prayer. Ask our Lady to obtain for you the grace to be faithful in prayer at all times, even when the going gets tough.

Jesus Will Cast Fire upon the Earth

Jesus said that He came to cast fire on the earth and that He is not at peace until that fire is enkindled. Paintings of the Sacred

Heart of Jesus and the Immaculate Heart of Mary depict those hearts surrounded by thorns but also with fire emanating from them. What does this fire symbolize? It symbolizes not only an overflowing love for all of us, but also a fervor and a passion for God through deep prayer. Jesus was not lukewarm or distracted in prayer. On the contrary, He prayed with all His heart, mind, body, and soul. What about you? How often has your prayer been done half-heartedly, with little fervor and faith? Do you lack fire?

Do this now: On Pentecost (after our Lady has been present with the Apostles in prayer for nine days) the Holy Spirit came down in tongues of fire to enlighten the minds of the Apostles and to set their hearts on fire with love of God and the desire to save souls. When you pray, humbly beseech our Lady for some of this fire so that you may consecrate yourself properly to Jesus through her in the coming days and all the days of your life.

Jesus Sweats Blood

Jesus atoned for us by taking all the sins of humanity upon Himself. In Gethsemane, like a deluge, the sins of the past, the sins of the present, and the sins of the future press down upon Him, and blood comes forth from His pores like sweat and trickles to the ground.

Do this now: With the eyes and the Heart of Mary, enter into the Sacred and sorrowful Heart of Jesus. With Our Lady, try to console Jesus in His mortal agony. Through our Lady's intercession, beg the Lord's pardon for all the sins of the world. Ask our Lady for true sorrow for your own sins and those of your family.

An Angel Consoles Jesus

In the midst of this intense sorrow, God the Father sends an angel to console Jesus.

> *Do this now*: As you contemplate this scene in prayer, ask our Lady for the grace to be like an angel of consolation to Jesus. Tell Jesus that you truly love Him and that you desire ardently to renounce everything in your life that has offended Him. As you console Him, implore our Lord to help you be more faithful to Him than you have ever been in your life. Beg Our Lady for the grace to grow in ever deeper friendship with Jesus.

Indifference

Unfortunately, one of the greatest sources of the sorrow that pierced the Heart of Jesus in His Sacred Passion is the cold indifference of so many souls, even many Catholics, and worse, many souls who have consecrated their lives to Jesus and His Kingdom. The book of Revelation warns us about indifference with these stark words: "I know your works: you are neither cold nor hot. Would that you were cold or hot! So, because you are lukewarm, and neither cold nor hot, I will spew you out of my mouth" (Rev. 3:15–16).

> *Do this now*: Sadness and discouragement often leave us indifferent to prayer, which we abandon because it seems to be having little effect. Saint Ignatius argues that such a response is the very opposite of the right one. When you are lukewarm or even desolate, he teaches, you should be exceptionally faithful to prayer, meditation, examination of conscience, and even add a little penance to conquer the moods. This is spiritual warfare, which you will be engaged in until the end of your life.

Finally, beg Jesus for the fire of love

What pierces the Hearts of Jesus and Mary profoundly is an attitude of coldness, indifference, apathy—a "whatever" or "who cares" attitude toward God and His Kingdom. As your consecration approaches, may our Lady obtain for you true repentance for your sins and a passion for Jesus and His Kingdom and for the salvation of souls. Remember that one soul is worth more than the whole created universe!

Day 2: Second Sorrowful Mystery

THE SCOURGING AT THE PILLAR

John 19:1
Read slowly and prayerfully

Then Pilate took Jesus and scourged him.

Meditate on the Scourging

Even though Jesus was innocent of any crime, the Roman procurator, Pontius Pilate, had Jesus scourged at the pillar to placate the crowd. By far, the most painful method of scourging was by means of what is called the Roman flagellum, a tool that was concocted in hell by the devil himself. It consists of a wooden handle with two or three leather thongs attached at the end, each thong knotted with pieces of metal and animal bones sharp as knives designed to remove quickly the flesh from the victim's body. The soldiers beat Jesus with this cruel instrument, inflicting pain beyond description. Just thinking of this atrocious suffering makes civilized souls cringe with fear.

Consider thoughtfully

Be Present at the Scourging

Mel Gibson's film *The Passion of the Christ* graphically depicts the scourging of Jesus at the pillar. It also shows how our Lady participated in her Son's Passion. The Blessed Virgin Mary as well as Saint Mary Magdalene are present at this piteous scene, seeing with their eyes, hearing with their ears, and suffering in their hearts what is happening to Jesus.

> *Do this now*: Compassion means a willingness to *suffer with* those we love. Our Lady has a truly compassionate heart and wants to attain for us a loving and compassionate heart like hers. Beg for the grace, through the intercession of Our Lady of Sorrows, to be spiritually present at the scourging of Jesus. Seeing how much Jesus suffered for our sake will render you better able to suffer for others who need your help and your compassion.

Christ Is Wounded for Our Offenses

The soldiers continue whipping, and the flesh of Jesus is continually ripped brutally from His Sacred Body. The executioners relish seeing an innocent man suffer such cruel torments. In all this intense suffering Jesus submits His will to that of His Heavenly Father, as He prayed in Gethsemane: "My Father, if it be possible, let this cup pass from me; nevertheless, not as I will, but as thou wilt" (Matt. 26:39).

> *Do this now*: The food of Jesus and the desire of the Immaculate Heart of Mary was to do the will of the Heavenly Father. Pray that as you move closer to the day of your consecration, you will develop in your heart an ever more intense and enduring desire to do the Father's will.

Jesus Suffers Massive Blood Loss

The cruel, barbarous soldiers act like wild animals as they take turns whipping Jesus, watching the instruments tear His flesh and cause blood to pour forth from His wounds. Our Lady must witness this, and, if we are to grasp fully the sacrifices Jesus made for us, so should we.

Do this now: Again, be present with the Blessed Virgin Mary and Saint Mary Magdalene in witnessing this horrendous scene, even though doing so is excruciatingly painful. Jesus and Mary suffered these pains because of their great love for us. Ask our Lady for the grace to suffer with her and to suffer with Jesus!

Why Jesus Suffered So Much

According to Saint John Paul II and a host of other saints, sins against the virtue of holy purity are the primary reason Jesus suffered the cruel torment of the scourging. These are sins that produce intense illicit or forbidden pleasure. In reparation for these many and serious sins, Jesus took it upon Himself to undergo the scourging in His mortal flesh. How great is the love of Jesus for us and His willingness to undergo a cruel treatment that almost makes us faint just to think about it!

Do this now: Try to enter into this piteous scene and, with fervor and intense prayer, strive to console Jesus and Mary. Beg pardon for all the sins of impurity throughout the world. How many sins — today more than ever — are committed against the virtue of purity!

Modesty in Dress

The scourging caused not only intense physical suffering but also great humiliation, for before the scourging Jesus was stripped of

His garments. This humiliation highlights the importance of modesty in the way we dress. In Portugal, Our Lady of Fatima warned that many fashions—referring to immodesty—would enter the world and offend God seriously. She also said that most souls were lost forever to the eternal fires of hell due to sins against the virtue of purity.

Do this now: Now is the time to examine your conscience about purity. Do you dress modestly at all times? Do you insist that your daughters always dress modestly? Or are you negligent and just go with the flow of modern worldly values? Do you realize that through immodesty in dress, you or your daughters may be an occasion of sin to many and may be wounding the hearts of Jesus and Mary gravely?

Finally, commit yourself anew to purity

Now is the time through the powerful intercession of our Lady and her most pure and Immaculate Heart to commit yourself to a life of purity. If you have the misfortune of falling into any sin against purity, arise and return to the Lord with a sincere and contrite heart through a good sacramental confession. Remember that God is slow to anger and rich in kindness to all who turn to Him and trust in His infinite mercy. Jesus said: "Blessed are the pure in heart, for they shall see God" (Matt. 5:8). May you cultivate purity of mind, thought, body, heart, desire, and intention in this life, so that you will contemplate the beauty of the faces of Jesus and Mary in heaven for all eternity!

THE CROWNING WITH THORNS

Matthew 27:28–31
Read slowly and prayerfully

And they stripped him and put a scarlet robe upon him, and plaiting a crown of thorns they put it on his head, and put a reed in his right hand. And kneeling before him they mocked him, saying, "Hail, King of the Jews!" And they spat upon him, and took the reed and struck him on the head. And when they had mocked him, they stripped him of the robe, and put his own clothes on him, and led him away to crucify him.

Meditate on the Crowning with Thorns

Jesus told Saint Faustina that holiness is measured by the willingness to suffer for the one you love. Aside from Jesus Himself, nobody ever suffered more than His Blessed Mother. She suffered with Jesus for us — for our conversion, our sanctification, our perseverance in grace, and our eternal salvation. No wonder Saint Ignatius insists that when we contemplate the Passion and suffering of Jesus we must beg for the grace to suffer with Jesus, to contemplate His crowning with thorns with the eyes, mind, and heart of the Blessed Virgin Mary.

Consider thoughtfully

Jesus Dragged and Mocked

Jesus has already been brutally scourged at the pillar, a beating that caused Him to lose much blood. After His scourging, He is bound and dragged to a place where He will spend the night and be tortured by brutal, merciless men. He is forced to sit on a stone while the soldiers mock and humiliate Him.

Do this now: Stay close to our Lady and see how much Jesus suffers for love of us and for the salvation of our souls. Talk to Jesus about His humiliations and console Him along with Mary, Our Lady of Sorrows.

The Face of Jesus

In his writing on the Blessed Virgin Mary and the Rosary, Saint John Paul II invites us to contemplate our Lady meditating on the face of Jesus in its various forms: the face of Jesus within her womb, the face of the Baby Jesus, the face of Jesus as a child, and the face of Jesus as a man. Remember, however, that our Lady also contemplated the sorrowful and anguished face of Jesus during His Passion.

Do this now: Join our Lady in contemplating the face of Jesus being spat upon, slapped, punched, and mocked.

Jesus Is Blindfolded

The humiliations and sufferings go on. The eyes of Jesus, the eyes that Mary gave Him, the most beautiful, pure, innocent, and loving of eyes, are blindfolded. Although Jesus Himself is the Light of the World, the blindfold deprives His own eyes of the light of day.

Do this now: Contemplate how Jesus, the Son of Mary, accepts the humiliation of not being able to see in order to give us spiritual sight through the light of faith, of truth, and of eternal salvation. Appeal to Mary under one of the many titles that associate her with light, such as Star of the Sea (*Stella Maris*), Star of the Morning (*Stella Matutina*), or Star of the New Evangelization.

Jesus Is Crowned with Thorns

The humiliations reach their climax when one of the torturers follows a satanic temptation to mock Jesus by crowning Him as King. They weave a crown of sharp thorns and shove it on his head so that the thorns penetrate his holy flesh. In all this Jesus remains silent as prophesied by Isaiah the prophet: "Like a lamb that is led to the slaughter, and like a sheep that before its shearers is dumb, so he opened not his mouth" (Isa. 53:7).

Do this now: With the eyes and heart of Mary, watch these brutal men press the sharp crown of thorns upon Jesus' brow. Contemplate the thorns digging deep into His flesh, causing a profuse loss of blood.

Jesus Is Mocked

For a "scepter," the executioners thrust a stick into Jesus' hands. Then they kneel before Him, making fun of Him as a mock king, yet He is truly the King of the universe. Mockery is essentially an act of the mind rather than of the body.

Do this now: With Our Lady, bow your mind, your heart, your will, and your soul to Jesus, acknowledging Him as the true king of your heart. Beg His pardon for the times you have sinned through the abuse of your mind, for letting bad thoughts take possession of your mind: lust, envy, jealousy, anger, greed, revenge, pride, rivalry. Look at Jesus' suffering, and resolve always to use your mind—memory, understanding, imagination—to glorify God and to save souls.

Finally, crown Jesus King of your life

The crowning with thorns is a cruel parody and mockery of Jesus as King. In reparation, resolve to crown Him as King of your life. May Jesus reign forever as your eternal King! May our Lady reign forever as your Queen! Enter now into deep conversation with our Lady over what you have been meditating upon. Talk to her about your own crowning with thorns. Maybe you have gone through sufferings, humiliations, scorn, and derision. Perhaps you are still wounded and angry over this maltreatment. Speak to our Lady. She will listen to you. She understands you. She will console you. She is your Mother! Through her presence and prayers you will start the very important process of healing. Among the many beautiful titles of our Lady is Health of the Sick. May her prayers touch the deep wounds in your heart and heal you.

Day 4: Fourth Sorrowful Mystery

JESUS CARRIES THE CROSS

John 19:17
Read slowly and prayerfully

So they took Jesus, and he went out, bearing his own cross, to the place called the place of a skull, which is called in Hebrew "Golgotha."

Meditate on the Way of the Cross

After Jesus is scourged and crowned with sharp thorns, He has to face the worst of all deaths — crucifixion — before which He has to carry His cross to Golgotha, the place of crucifixion. As He begins to carry His heavy cross, He falls; other falls soon follow. He has lost much blood; He is exhausted. He knows that once He reaches the summit of Calvary, the worst yet awaits Him: the crucifixion with nails that will pierce His hands and His feet. Then Jesus experiences both sorrow and consolation — He meets His Blessed and Sorrowful Mother. Jesus and Mary, the sinless and the innocent, suffer for our guilt and sin. How great is their love for us!

Consider thoughtfully

Mary Follows Jesus Bearing the Cross

Among many unforgettable scenes in Mel Gibson's *The Passion of the Christ* is Jesus carrying the Cross. The film presents our Lady following Jesus the whole way; Satan is on the other side, with his ugly, sarcastic look. Our Lady is faithful to Jesus until the very end.

Do this now: Through the intercession of our Lady, humbly beg for the grace to walk faithfully with her and Jesus on the way to Calvary. What do you think went on in their hearts? Try to be present with our Lady as she contemplates her Son Jesus about to be crucified. Ponder this; contemplate this; pray over this.

His Friends Abandon Him

It is easy to be faithful to a friend when the sun is shining, the birds are singing, the gentle spring breeze caresses your face. It is easy to be faithful to a friend at a party, in joy and celebration. But when the friend encounters crisis, suffering, and failure, many take to their heels and leave him alone. Most of the Apostles left Jesus when He most needed them, mainly due to fear. Our Lady was there when Jesus most needed her presence. She was faithful to the end.

Do this now: Beg our Lady for *faithfulness* to Jesus, for *compassion* toward Jesus and others (especially those in your family), and for *heroic patience* with God, self, and others (again, especially those in your family). Most especially, beg her for *great love for Jesus*, who willingly carried His Cross, loaded with all the sins of humanity, including your sins, because He loves you so much.

Jesus and Mary Meet Again

Sorrow increases in the Heart of Jesus, but with it an immense joy. Why? For the simple reason that He meets the person in the world who loves Him most, cares for Him most, and is willing to suffer most with Him. Their eyes meet.

Do this now: Contemplate this encounter and then enter into conversation with both Jesus and Mary. Tell them how much you treasure what they went through for love of you. Tell them how sorry and repentant you are for your past sins; reassert your willingness to give up your sins in the future.

Jesus Has Infinite Patience

We all struggle with patience in our lives. See Jesus carrying the Cross, loaded down with all the sins of the world, from those of Adam and Eve to those of the very last person at the end of time. See how willingly and patiently Jesus carries the Cross. Our Lady is present with Him, helping Him carry the Cross by the immensity of love that flows from her Sorrowful and Immaculate Heart.

Do this now: Contemplating this scene, talk to Jesus and Mary about a constant problem that plagues you — and your impatience. Beg for patience in the different aspects of your life.

♦ *Pray for your spouse*: Mother Mary, help me to support the limitations of my spouse. Instead of criticizing him/her, help me to pray for him/her and support him/her by my presence! May I imitate the saints, especially Saint Monica!

♦ *Pray for your children*: Mother Mary, help my children turn back to Jesus if they have turned away from Him.

They have chosen to carry false crosses that will only bring them misery. Help them turn back to Jesus, who is meek and humble of heart.

♦ *Pray for patience during health problems*: Mother Mary, help me to carry the cross of this health issue that causes me so much pain, fear, and anxiety. Help me to carry this in union with the Cross of Jesus. Help me to offer it for the conversion, sanctification, and salvation of my family.

♦ *Pray for the healing of memories*: Mother Mary, I am carrying crosses from my past—wounds and memories that surface like phantoms to torture me. Please free me from their pain.

♦ *Pray for a richer prayer life*: Mother Mary, model of contemplation and action, help me to be patient with my daily prayer life. Help me not to depend so much on feelings but be guided by faith and reason. Help me to persevere until the end.

♦ *Pray for better social relations*: Mother Mary, help me to be patient with this person who causes me so much suffering and grief. Ask God to grant me patience as I contemplate your Divine Son carrying His heavy Cross.

♦ *Pray that you may bear your work better*: Mother Mary, my work is a trial and a cross for me. Help me to do the ordinary tasks of my daily life with extraordinary love in imitation of you.

♦ *Pray for relief from monotony and boredom*: Mother Mary, routine and the grind of daily life are a heavy cross to me. Help me to cultivate a supernatural perspective in all that I do. May I accept the cross of the boredom and monotony of daily life for the salvation of my soul and the souls of my loved ones.

♦ *Pray for ailing family members and others*: Mother Mary, the cross of dealing with sick and suffering family members is sometimes beyond my strength. Be there with me that I may see Jesus on the Cross and Jesus crucified in suffering humanity. "As you did it to one of the least of these my brethren, you did it to me" (Matt. 25:40). Dear Mary, help me to see Jesus in all others, especially those who suffer the most and those who are marginalized in society.

♦ *Pray that you may age gracefully*: Help me, dear Mother Mary, to accept the cross of aging. This, too, I willingly accept as part of my cross and as a means to my salvation.

Finally, turn to Mary yet again

Dear Mary, as I contemplate you with Jesus carrying the heavy Cross on His shoulder, help me to carry all my crosses so that one day I may participate in the glory of the resurrection. Ask God to give me the wisdom and strength to grow in faith, love, and devotion as I prepare for my consecration to Jesus though you!

THE CRUCIFIXION

John 19:25–30
Read slowly and prayerfully

Standing by the cross of Jesus were his mother, and his mother's sister, Mary the wife of Clopas, and Mary Magdalene. When Jesus saw his mother, and the disciple whom he loved standing near, he said to his mother, "Woman, behold, your son!" Then he said to the disciple, "Behold, your mother!" And from that hour the disciple took her to his own home.

After this Jesus, knowing that all was now finished, said (to fulfil the scripture), "I thirst." A bowl full of vinegar stood there; so they put a sponge full of the vinegar on hyssop and held it to his mouth. When Jesus had received the vinegar, he said, "It is finished"; and he bowed his head and gave up his spirit.

Meditate on the Crucifixion

Weighed down with the sins of humanity—including your sins and mine—Jesus reaches the top of Mount Calvary. Crucifixion awaits Him. Our Lady is present to witness the crucifixion of her only Son. As Jesus willingly hangs on the Cross, our Lady looks at Him, mostly in silence! She sees His Precious Blood ooze forth from His sacred head crowned with thorns; from His hands pierced with sharp nails; from His sacred body brutally scourged only hours earlier, with wounds reopened when He was stripped of His garments; from His sacred feet, which for three years brought the Good News to the poor and the afflicted and which are now nailed to the Cross of our sins.

Consider thoughtfully

Mary Is Compassionate

Mary has compassion—a total willingness to suffer with Jesus. "Greater love has no man than this, that a man lay down his life for his friends" (John 15:13). Our Lady wanted to suffer with her dying Son for love of Him and also for love of all of humanity, and that means for you and me.

Do this now: Humbly ask for the grace to accompany our Lady, the Mother of Sorrows, in the last hours of the life of her Son. Beg for the grace to enter the depths of the Immaculate and Sorrowful Heart of Mary and to feel as far as possible what she felt. With your eyes, contemplate the Lord Jesus being crucified, and allow it to penetrate your heart as well.

Nails Pierce Jesus' Hands and Feet

The brutal executioners pound nails into Jesus' hands, and His Blood comes forth—the Precious Blood that was given to Him through Mary. Nails pierced His feet.

Do this now: With our Lady at your side, contemplate with great love the anguish and pain manifested in the sacred face of Jesus—the sacred face that our Lady tenderly caressed and kissed when Jesus was a baby. Be close to Mary and try to console her with your words and your compassionate presence.

Three Remain Faithful

After they nail Jesus to the Cross, they lift the Cross high, leaving Jesus to hang there for three long hours. At the foot of the Cross for the whole time are the faithful three—Mary Magdalene, Saint John the Evangelist, and the Blessed Virgin Mary. But there is a fourth person mystically present—that is you!

Do this now: Take your place now with John, Mary Magdalene, and our Lady. Draw close to our Lady as she shares in the Passion, suffering, and death of our Lord and Savior, Jesus Christ. Be with Jesus as He suffers, and thank Him for the gift of salvation. Stay close to our Lady; talk to her; console her in her mortal anguish. Beg for the grace of being faithful until the end.

Jesus Speaks to Mary, to St. John, and to You

Jesus' energy and strength are quickly declining. His blood loss is great, and His breathing is labored as He approaches His last minutes on the Cross. Despite His suffering, Jesus loves all the more intensely. He peers down from the Cross and sees His two greatest lovers and friends: His dear Mother and Saint John. Before dying, Jesus wants to leave His Mother with His best friend—John the Beloved.

Do this now: Imagine that you are present at the foot of the Cross with our Lady, with Mary Magdalene, and with

John the Beloved. Listen to the words that Jesus addresses to His Mother and to John, and also to you: "'Woman, behold, your son!' … 'Behold, your mother!' And from that hour the disciple took her to his own home." (John 19:26–27). In the person of John, Jesus gives Mary as our universal Mother: Mary is the Mother of God, the Mother of the Church, and the Mother of all of humanity. Most important, she is the Mother of you and of me!

Mary Is Your Mother, Too

Mary indeed is your Mother by Jesus' own words from the Cross. Your relationship to Mary as Mother must transform your life totally! As your spiritual Mother, Mary will act in a most powerful way in your life. As your Mother, she cares for you, prays for you, understands you deeply, and watches over you at all times. Her love for you goes way beyond your limited understanding.

Do this now: In *The Glories of Mary*, Saint Alphonsus Liguori expresses the fathomless depth of our Lady's love for you individually and personally. Meditate upon his words: "If we heaped together all the love that mothers have for their children, all the love of husbands and wives, all the love of all the angels and saints for their clients, it could never equal Mary's love for even a single soul." How immense is Mary's love for you!

Finally, Speak to Mary as Your Mother

Talk to your heavenly Mother! Dig into the depths of your heart and reveal your most intimate desires and secrets to her.

Our Lady, your loving and tender Mother, will hear you and respond to your prayers. Fear nothing! Remember that our Lady knows you, understands you, and loves you beyond your wildest imaginings.

First and Second Repetitions

On days 6 and 7 repeat one of the mysteries on which you meditated this week. You might choose a meditation during which God moved you and poured abundant consolations into your soul. There may be more consolations waiting for you. Like a bee that returns to a flower for more nectar, return to the flower of this meditation for more spiritual nectar.

St. Ignatius suggests that sometimes it's good to choose a meditation during which you experienced desolation. Why? Desolation in prayer often manifests a certain resistance on our part to grace. Ask the Holy Spirit to help you break down that resistance through repetition.

Enter into the meditation, beginning with the steps found on pages 10 and 11. Then say this prayer:

> *We adore You, O Christ*
> *And we praise You,*
> *Because by Your holy Cross*
> *You have redeemed the world!*

Week 4

THE GLORIOUS MYSTERIES

Day 1: First Glorious Mystery

THE RESURRECTION

Mark 16:1–8
Read slowly and prayerfully

And when the sabbath was past, Mary Magdalene, and Mary the mother of James, and Salome, bought spices, so that they might go and anoint him. And very early on the first day of the week they went to the tomb when the sun had risen. And they were saying to one another, "Who will roll away the stone for us from the door of the tomb?" And looking up, they saw that the stone was rolled back; for it was very large. And entering the tomb, they saw a young man sitting on the right side, dressed in a white robe; and they were amazed. And he said to them, "Do not be amazed; you seek Jesus of Nazareth, who was crucified. He has risen, he is not here; see the place where they laid him. But go, tell his disciples and Peter that he is going before you to Galilee; there you will see him, as he told you." And they went out and fled from the tomb; for trembling and astonishment had come upon them; and they said nothing to any one, for they were afraid.

Meditate on the Risen Jesus

The culminating point of our faith is the Resurrection of Our Lord and Savior, Jesus Christ. He was crucified, died, and was buried; the third day He rose from the dead. The Paschal Mystery includes these key elements: His Passion (suffering), His death on the Cross, and His burial in the tomb. Finally, Jesus truly rose from the dead, sharing with us His life and eternal life!

Consider thoughtfully

Sorrow and Joy

Aside from Jesus Himself nobody on earth ever suffered more than Mary, the Sorrowful Mother. For that reason our Lady is also hailed as Queen of Martyrs. At the same time nobody ever experienced more joy in this world than our Lady. As you can never fully understand her sorrow, so you can never fathom the immensity of the overflowing joy that she experienced because of the Resurrection of Jesus. No wonder she is called the Cause of our Joy!

Do this now: Implore Mary for the grace to come to know, love, and trust Jesus as she did. Although she was devastated by His death and burial, she never ceased to trust in God and hope for the future. Beg Mary to help you develop the virtues of hope and trust.

Mary Expected Jesus' Resurrection

Although our Lady suffered most, she never doubted that Jesus would rise from the dead. She had deep faith and sure hope that she would see her risen Son Jesus the Lord.

Do this now: As you journey toward your consecration, ask Mary to help you develop a profound faith in the power of the Resurrection of Jesus in your life, and hope, which is like an anchor. "Hail, holy Queen, mother of mercy, our life, our sweetness, and our hope."

Our Lady Meets Jesus after the Resurrection

Imagine our Lady in the days after the Crucifixion. She still suffers the grief of having lost the treasure of her life—her Son, Lord, God, and Savior—yet she also believes that He will rise from the dead. Her hope is like an anchor; it is very firm. Then Jesus, the Light of the Dawn, comes to visit her. It is their first meeting after His Resurrection.

Do this now: Ask the Holy Spirit for the grace to be able to imagine and contemplate the appearance of Jesus to Mary after His Resurrection from the dead. Beg for this grace!

Jesus Appears to Our Lady

Jesus appears in His glorified and risen body and approaches His Mother. "Shalom!" This is the typical Jewish greeting, which means: "Peace be with you!" Mary arises from where she was praying and contemplates her glorified Son, the treasure of her life. Jesus embraces her. Tears of overflowing joy fill her eyes and roll down her cheeks. Jesus consoles and encourages Mary after all she has gone through out of love for Him, as well as for her love for the Church, the Mystical Body of Christ.

Do this now: Be present at this loving encounter. Talk to both Jesus and Mary. Pour out your heart. Tell our Lady of your own interior struggles and sorrows. She will understand you better than you could ever imagine. Ask Jesus for consolation and encouragement.

His Wounds Are Signs of Love

Our Lady contemplates the wounds of Jesus, peering into the holes left by the nails that pierced His hands. She contemplates Jesus' feet, which had brought the Good News of salvation to the poor, and sees that they also are pierced through. Finally, she contemplates the large, gaping wound in Jesus' side, where, after Jesus died, the soldier had thrust his lance. Jesus' most Sacred Heart was pierced with the lance, and blood and water came gushing forth. These wounds are signs of Jesus' love for all of humanity, including you and me.

Do this now: Consecration to Jesus through Mary invites you to contemplate the wounds of Jesus and especially His most Sacred Heart, pierced with the lance. As you contemplate this scene of the Risen Jesus appearing to Mary and consoling her, open your heart more and more to her and reveal to her what is going on in the depths of your heart.

Jesus Opened the Gates of Heaven

Jesus, the Son of Mary, truly rose from the dead. The reason? To open the gates of heaven for you and for me so that at the end of this short time on earth, this valley of tears, we will be with Jesus, Mary, the angels, and the saints in heaven forever.

Do this now: Beseech our Lady, through the grace of the Risen Lord, to give you an ardent and earnest yearning for eternal life!

Finally, beg for the joy of the Resurrection

As you move closer to the day of your consecration of your whole life to Jesus through our Lady, ask that through her intercession you may be granted the most intense joy. May our Lady help you to understand that true joy does not come from material things, honor, wealth, power, or pleasure. May she teach you that true joy comes from encountering Jesus, knowing Him, and loving Him! Our Lady teaches us this in her prayer the Magnificat: "My soul magnifies the Lord, and my spirit rejoices in God my Savior" (Luke 1:46–47).

Day 2: Second Glorious Mystery

THE ASCENSION OF JESUS INTO HEAVEN

Mark 16:15–20
Read slowly and prayerfully

He said to them, "Go into all the world and preach the gospel to the whole creation. He who believes and is baptized will be saved; but he who does not believe will be condemned. And these signs will accompany those who believe: in my name they will cast out demons; they will speak in new tongues; they will pick up serpents, and if they drink any deadly thing, it will not hurt them; they will lay their hands on the sick, and they will recover."

So then the Lord Jesus, after he had spoken to them, was taken up into heaven, and sat down at the right hand of God. And they went forth and preached everywhere, while the Lord worked with them and confirmed the message by the signs that attended it.

Meditate on our call to heaven

We were created to know God, to love God, and to serve God in this life so as to be forever with Him in heaven. Heaven is the goal of our existence. Our Lady can play a key role in praying for us and helping us to desire God and heaven above all created realities, even life itself!

Consider thoughtfully

Heaven Is Our True Home

Before ascending into heaven, Jesus reassured the Apostles with these promising words: "In my Father's house are many rooms; if it were not so, would I have told you that I go to prepare a place for you? And when I go and prepare a place for you, I will come again and will take you to myself, that where I am you may be also" (John 14:2–3).

Do this now: Jesus ascended into heaven to prepare a place for us. Our Lady is also in heaven with her Son, Jesus. Both Jesus and Mary are our best friends, and they are waiting for us in heaven. Contemplate the reality of heaven. This is the goal of your life, the goal of your existence! Beg our Lady that you will be saved and be in heaven forever with her.

Mary's Relation to the Trinity

Our Lady has a special relation to God. She is the daughter of God the Father the Mother of God the Son, and the Mystical Spouse of the Holy Spirit. Therefore, Our Lady is intimately connected and interrelated to the Blessed Trinity — Father, Son, and Holy Spirit. That means in concrete that to forge a deeper relationship with God as our Father, we want to turn to our Lady. To cultivate a deeper relationship with Jesus, who received His humanity from Mary, our Lady is the key. Finally, our Lady is also the way to grow closer to the Holy Spirit.

Do this now: Talk to Mary and then talk to God the Father; talk to Mary and then talk to God the Son; talk to Mary and then talk to God the Holy Spirit. Our Lady is the gateway to union with the Blessed Trinity.

Mary's Relation to the Angels

Angels, archangels, virtues, powers, dominions, cherubim, and seraphim—all the choirs of angels sing out in praise of God for giving them our Lady as their queen and empress!

Do this now: A deeper relationship with Mary and consecration to her will help you enter into deeper relationship with your Guardian Angel and all of the angels. Talk to Mary about the angels and her relationship to them. Call upon your Guardian Angel to help prepare you for your coming consecration to Jesus through Mary.

Mary's Relation to the Saints

Mary has long been known as "Queen of All the Saints." The saints in heaven contemplate Mary as their queen, mother, guide, model, and inspiration. She is also their life, their sweetness, and their hope.

Do this now: Remember daily to pray to the saints for assistance, approaching in particular those for whom you have special affinity. Ask them to intercede with Mary and Jesus for you, and to help Mary become, as she was for the saints, your life, your sweetness, and your hope.

Mary's Relation to Confessors

Mary's title "Queen of Confessors" refers to the special favor she shows to those who courageously profess their Faith.

Do this now: In this age when few profess their Faith publicly, ask our Lady for the grace to know your Faith better and to profess it bravely.

Mary's Relation to Martyrs

Mary has long been known as the "Queen of Martyrs," a title that signifies her special love for those who sacrifice themselves for the Faith, whether by dying for it or living for it when a life of faith is very costly.

Do this now: Implore the Queen of Martyrs for the patience and fortitude you need to live out your Faith and to accept gracefully whatever sufferings God permits you to endure.

Mary's Relation to Virgins

Jesus said: "Blessed are the pure in heart, for they shall see God" (Matt. 5:8). In a world where there are so many temptations to give in to impurity in so many forms and manners, our Lady, Queen of Virgins, stands out as a shining star, a beautiful, untouched rose. It is through the powerful prayers of our Lady and a deep love for the Sacred Heart of Jesus that you will find yourself able to practice all virtues, but especially that of purity.

Do this now: Pray to our Lady for purity and preservation of our children and young people, and for purity in your marital commitment and in the sacrament of Holy Matrimony. Ask her to help you in the constant fight against the devils of immodesty, vulgarity, and the porn culture. May our Lady's most pure heart enclose and encompass you and those you love!

Mary's Relation to Priests, Bishops, and Religious

In heaven our Lady is also the queen of cardinals, bishops, priests, brothers, nuns, and all consecrated souls. Through her prayers many consecrated souls are given the grace to live more fully the vows of poverty, chastity, and obedience they have professed. Our Lady lived chastity perfectly; she was totally obedient to the Word of God and the will of God; she lived a life of total detachment from the things of this world! Her heart was totally set on God and all that belongs to Him and His Kingdom.

Do this now: Enter into conversation with our Lady now and ask her to intercede for more vocations to the religious life and to the priesthood. Jesus said: "The harvest is plentiful, but the laborers are few; pray therefore the Lord of the harvest to send out laborers into his harvest" (Matt. 9:37–38). May your prayers to our Lady inspire many young people to say yes to God!

Finally, visualize our Lady in heaven

The primary focus of this Marian meditation was to visualize our Lady in heaven and to ponder her unique role there. Heaven is waiting for all of us. Mary is praying in heaven for us right now. Have a deep conversation with our Lady, Queen of Angels and Queen of Saints. Ask her for a sincere desire to go to heaven.

Day 3: Third Glorious Mystery

THE COMING OF THE HOLY SPIRIT

Acts 2:1–11
Read slowly and prayerfully

When the day of Pentecost had come, they were all together in one place. And suddenly a sound came from heaven like the rush of a mighty wind, and it filled all the house where they were sitting. And there appeared to them tongues as of fire, distributed and resting on each one of them. And they were all filled with the Holy Spirit and began to speak in other tongues, as the Spirit gave them utterance.

Now there were dwelling in Jerusalem Jews, devout men from every nation under heaven. And at this sound the multitude came together, and they were bewildered, because each one heard them speaking in his own language. And they were amazed and wondered, saying, "Are not all these who are speaking Galileans? And how is it that we hear, each of us in his own native language? Parthians and Medes and Elamites and residents of Mesopotamia, Judea and Cappadocia, Pontus and Asia, Phrygia and Pamphylia, Egypt and the parts of Libya belonging to Cyrene, and visitors from Rome, both Jews and proselytes, Cretans and Arabians, we hear them telling in our own tongues the mighty works of God."

Meditate on Pentecost

At the end of the nine days and nights of prayer, fasting, and silence with the Blessed Virgin Mary, there was a powerful wind—almost like that of a tornado—that shook the whole house where they were. Tongues of fire descended over the heads of the Apostles, and they all were transformed, being filled with the Holy Spirit and apostolic zeal to go forth and preach the gospel to all nations. This was the birthday of the Church, facilitated by the prayers and presence of our Lady, who is the Mother of the Church. The closer you draw to Mary, the more fully the Holy Spirit will take control of your whole person.

Consider thoughtfully

Mary Is Queen of the Apostles
Jesus has ascended into heaven where He sits at the right hand of the Father, but before He ascended, He promised to send them the Paraclete, Consoler, Counselor, Friend, and Companion on the highway to heaven. Mary and the Apostles go to the Cenacle, known as the Upper Room, where they spend nine days and nights in silence, prayer, penance, and fasting.

Do this now: Contemplate our Lady at prayer. The Apostles did this, and it truly inspired them to pray more and to pray better. Our Lady can help us to grow in prayer, which is, of course, union with God. Contemplate the beautiful countenance of Mary. Humility, peace, serenity, purity, simplicity, transparency, docility, and sweetness — all of these characteristics reflect Our Lady absorbed in prayer. Try to imagine in contemplation the Apostles together with Mary at prayer. What a wonderful and inspiring scene. Try to truly be present there.

Mary's Prayers for the Salvation of Souls

What went on in the prayer of Mary? We do not have any exact certitude. We can certainly imagine, however, an overflowing love for the Father, the Son, and the Holy Spirit. Nobody loved the Trinity more than Mary! And because what God loves most is the salvation of souls, our Lady would certainly be praying for the salvation of souls.

Do this now: Turn your gaze to Mary and beg her for special graces. Ask her to help you love God with all of your heart, mind, soul, and strength. She can help you! Then implore her for apostolic zeal, a fervent desire to do all in your power to work for the salvation of immortal souls.

The Immaculate Conception

By means of the Holy Spirit, Mary was conceived without the stain of Original Sin. Devotion to Mary will instill in your mind, memory, intellect, and will the presence of the Holy Spirit, leaving you more detached from sin as you come to have the freedom of sons and daughters of God.

Do this now: As you prepare for your consecration, which draws nearer by the day, ask Mary to obtain for you an abundant outpouring of the Holy Spirit and the grace to live a purer and holier life.

The Different Languages at Pentecost

One of the many gifts bestowed upon the Apostles on Pentecost was the gift of languages: the ability to communicate clearly, powerfully, and convincingly to others the Word of God, the Word of salvation. This was a gratuitous and powerful gift that converted and saved many souls. Our Lady, who gave the world Jesus, the Word of God, was present and witnessed this transformation. May our Lady obtain for you the gift of eloquence in spiritual matters.

Do this now: During the Last Supper, Jesus gave His Apostles this commandment: "Love one another as I have loved you" (John 15:12). Let us turn now to our Lady for the grace of communication with the language of love—the most important of all languages. Ask her to pray for you, that you may become a true apostle of our Lord and Savior, Jesus Christ. May our Lady's prayers motivate you—like the Apostles after Pentecost—to carry the Good News of salvation to the whole world. And never forget that words are most powerful when they are supported by the powerful example of your life.

♦ *Love your spouse*: Without the help of your spouse, it will be hard for your family to grow holy; but without your kind and attentive love, it will be hard for your spouse to help you in this critical effort. Ask Mary, the perfect spouse, to help you grow like her in love for your spouse, and pray that her intercession may lead your marriage to be holy like that of Mary and Joseph.

- *Love your children*: Charity begins at home. Ask our Lady to help inspire in you good words that your children are able to hear and accept, particularly the Word of God, and that your words and example may draw them finally to love Mary and join her forever in heaven.

- *Love others*: Like the Apostles, you will sometimes be sent to places and put in circumstances where you are called to give witness to the Risen Lord Jesus and the Gospel. Ask our Lady to pray that you will be always and everywhere a true instrument of salvation.

Finally, welcome the action of the Holy Spirit

The Apostles were transformed into fiery darts in the hands of our Lord. Before Pentecost, they had given in to fear and cowardice. After Pentecost, through the prayers of Mary and the coming of the Holy Spirit, they were radically transformed into saints. Welcome the Holy Spirit's action so that you may live a life of holiness and transform the world! May you say with St. Paul: "It is no longer I who live, but Christ who lives in me" (Gal. 2:20).

Day 4: Fourth Glorious Mystery

THE ASSUMPTION OF OUR LADY INTO HEAVEN

Revelation 12:1–6
Read slowly and prayerfully

And a great portent appeared in heaven, a woman clothed with the sun, with the moon under her feet, and on her head a crown of twelve stars; she was with child and she cried out in her pangs of birth, in anguish for delivery. And another portent appeared in heaven; behold, a great red dragon, with seven heads and ten horns, and seven diadems upon his heads. His tail swept down a third of the stars of heaven, and cast them to the earth. And the dragon stood before the woman who was about to bear a child, that he might devour her child when she brought it forth; she brought forth a male child, one who is to rule all the nations with a rod of iron, but her child was caught up to God and to his throne, and the woman fled into the wilderness, where she has a place prepared by God, in which to be nourished for one thousand two hundred and sixty days.

Meditate on the Assumption of Mary

The Joyful Mysteries radiate joy because Jesus comes into the world as Savior through the yes of the Blessed Virgin Mary. The Glorious Mysteries radiate and communicate great joy because both Jesus and Mary point to our ultimate and eternal destiny, which is Heaven. We were created to know, love, and serve God in this world so as to be with Him and Mary forever in heaven, praising God for all eternity. This thought should fill us with immense joy!

Consider thoughtfully

Mary's Whole Being Was Devoted to God
From the earliest days of her life to her last day on Earth, Mary used every part of her body to glorify God. In her life, she wasted nothing but used everything that God gave her His honor and glory and for the salvation of souls.

Do this now: Ask Mary for the grace to use your body in the most perfect way possible and, by making a strong effort to avoid sin, to avoid hurting yourself, others, and, of course, God.

Mary's Body
Sin is the worst enemy in our spiritual life. Our Lady was sinless from the moment of her conception and throughout her life; she is the sinless one in heaven.

Do this now: Mary's mind was filled with light — the Holy Spirit. Her eyes were primarily used to focus on all the aspects of Jesus' life. Ask our Lady to help you use your body and all its faculties and members to glorify God on earth and forever in heaven.

Mary's Mind
The Apostle Saint Paul says, "We have the mind of Christ" (1 Cor. 2:16). What a marvelous truth! Mary gave Jesus His physical body, which means that the very mind of Jesus—His memory, understanding, and imagination—was formed within her womb.

Do this now: The minds of Jesus and of Mary were perfect. Ask God to form your mind to be as much like theirs as is humanly possible, so that you may always glorify God with your mind.

Mary's Memory
Like our Lady, we should use our memory to recall the Word of God, which should be a lamp for our steps and a light for our path, and to dwell on holy, wholesome, and edifying memories that are worthy of God and His Kingdom.

Do this now: Implore our Lady to help you make frequent confessions so as to purify your memory of past hurtful, impure, and unholy thoughts!

Mary's Understanding
Neither Jesus nor Mary was stained by Original Sin or afflicted with its consequences. Their minds were clear and transparent, bright, strong, and highly intelligent, and open always to the operation of the Holy Spirit.

Do this now: Turn to both Jesus and Mary, begging them for a strong, intelligent, and lucid intellect so that you will be able to absorb and love the truth and to put it into practice. The truth will set you free!

The Thought Is Father to the Deed

Thoughts lead to decisions; decisions lead to sentiments; sentiments lead to firm decisions; firm decisions lead to actions; repeated actions form habits; habits form personality; finally, personality determines your destiny for all eternity.

Do this now: Now and often during the day, call to mind the words of Saint Paul: "We have the mind of Christ."

Mary's Eyes and Your Eyes

Jesus said in one of the Beatitudes: "Blessed are the pure in heart, for they shall see God" (Matt. 5:8). For just over thirty years, our Lady's dearest treasure was Jesus, her only Son. She contemplated Jesus as a baby in her arms and as a little toddler in their home in Nazareth. She watched intently as Jesus grew in age, wisdom, and strength before God and man. She contemplated Jesus as a young man working hard for long hours in the carpenter shop of good Saint Joseph. She contemplated Jesus with her eyes as well as with her Immaculate Heart.

Do this now: Mary's greatest joy and delight was to be with Jesus. She spent time watching Him, contemplating every one of His sacred actions. On earth, her eyes and her Immaculate Heart were totally fixed on Jesus, as they are now that she is in heaven. Turn your attention to the beauty of Mary in heaven. Dwell on the beauty of her eyes as she contemplates the majesty of the Blessed Trinity.

Finally, ask for the proper use of your body

As your total consecration to Jesus and Mary approaches, ask our Lady, assumed into heaven, to intercede for the grace to use your entire body to glorify God. In a special way, beg our Lady for the grace to control your eyes—to avoid offending God by looking at persons, images, screens, and places that could so easily dirty and tarnish your eyes as well as your immortal soul.

THE CROWNING OF MARY AS QUEEN OF HEAVEN AND EARTH

Revelation 12:1
Read slowly and prayerfully

And a great portent appeared in heaven, a woman clothed with the sun, with the moon under her feet, and on her head a crown of twelve stars.

Meditate on Mary's crowning in heaven

The crowning of Mary as Queen of Heaven and Earth is truly a glorious mystery. After our Lady is taken up, body and soul, into heaven comes the moment of her glorious crowning. Picture the beauty of the Queen! The Eternal Father, with the Son (Jesus the King) is placing the most beautiful crown imaginable on Mary's head. The crown is filled with diamonds, rubies, emeralds, and many other precious gems. The angels look on in joy; the saints contemplate with their hearts filled with love. A glorious song of praise erupts from the angelic choirs and the saint's realm. For all eternity, our Lady will have this beautiful, awe-inspiring crown on her head. This crown will never fall, never become rusty or tarnished, and never collect dust. It will always shine!

Consider thoughtfully

Mary, Queen of Virgins

In a world in which the virtue of purity is severely attacked even from the youngest years, we must lift our eyes to Mary, who is the Queen of Virgins.

Do this now: Contemplate the beauty of the Queen of Heaven and Earth and beg her for special graces in the realm of purity. Say the following prayer: "Mary, most pure Virgin, Queen of Heaven and Earth, attain for me the precious jewel that you treasured so dearly all of your life—the jewel of purity! Dear Lady and Queen, attain for me purity of eyes so that, like you, I might contemplate the beauty and glory of God in all of creation and in all of the persons He created. Jesus taught us: 'Blessed are the pure in heart, for they shall see God': Mother most pure, attain for me a pure mind—including memory, understanding, and imagination. Help me, in the words of Saint Paul, to put on the mind of Christ. You gave Jesus His mind; help me to imitate more and more the mind of Christ in all of my thoughts. Dear Mary, attain for me a pure body that all of my actions might be pleasing to God and to you. Help me to recognize my dignity from the moment of my creation and from my Baptism. Dear Mary, help me to recognize that my body is the temple of the Holy Spirit and is destined for eternal beatitude. Dear Mary, Virgin most holy, grant me a most pure heart so as to love God fully, totally, and unreservedly! Grant me also purity of intention, that all I do might be done for the honor and glory of God and for the salvation of countless souls. Amen."

Mary, Queen of Martyrs

The martyrs were given the grace to shed their blood—in imitation of Jesus, the King of Martyrs—for the sake of truth or for the sake of defending a virtue. As Saint Alphonsus Liguori points out, the sword that pierced the heart of Jesus also penetrated the soul and heart of our Lady. For that reason, our Lady is known as the Queen of Martyrs.

Do this now: In this world in which we are surrounded by so much evil—in politics, the economy, erroneous teaching, and satanic practices—now more than ever we urgently need strength to be faithful to Jesus and Mary to the very end of the fight! Beg our Lady, Queen of Martyrs, to attain for you the grace to be strong in confronting temptations, trials, tribulations, afflictions, and possibly martyrdom.

Our Lady's Great Desire

Our Lady, Queen of Heaven and Earth, has a very special but ardent desire. She wants another special jewel to be placed in the center of her crown, a jewel that she will treasure for all eternity—that jewel is you! Yes, she desires most ardently to have you with her in heaven as one of the most glorious human jewels embedded in her crown. She wants you to be there for all eternity.

Do this now: Beseech our Lady, Queen of Heaven and Earth, for the grace to be worthy of one day being one of those most precious jewels embedded in her crown for all eternity. Pray fervently to her for the grace to imitate her most sublime virtues: deep humility, lively faith, blind obedience, unceasing prayer, constant self-denial, surpassing purity, ardent love, heroic patience, angelic kindness, and heavenly wisdom (see Saint Louis de Montfort, *True Devotion to Mary*, no. 108 — the ten virtues of Mary).

Finally, pray the Hail, Holy Queen

As you conclude your meditation on our Lady, Queen of Angels and Saints, Queen of Virgins and Confessors and Martyrs, Queen of All Hearts, pray this glorious prayer in honor of Mary as Queen:

> Hail, holy Queen, Mother of mercy, our life, our sweetness, and our hope. To thee do we cry, poor banished children of Eve. To thee do we send up our sighs, mourning, and weeping in this valley of tears. Turn, then, most gracious advocate, thine eyes of mercy toward us, and after this, our exile, show unto us the blessed fruit of thy womb, Jesus. O clement, O loving, O sweet Virgin Mary.
>
> V. Pray for us, O holy Mother of God.
>
> R. That we may be made worthy of the promises of Christ.
>
> May our Lady, the queen of your heart, obtain for you abundant mercy and eternal life; perpetual sweetness even in the midst of the many bitter moments of life; and total hope and trust in God's loving providence all the days of your life.

THE FIRST MIRACLE OF JESUS

John 2:1–11
Read slowly and prayerfully

On the third day there was a marriage at Cana in Galilee, and
the mother of Jesus was there; Jesus also was invited to the marriage, with his disciples. When the wine failed, the mother of
Jesus said to him, "They have no wine." And Jesus said to her,
"O woman, what have you to do with me? My hour has not yet
come." His mother said to the servants, "Do whatever he tells
you." Now six stone jars were standing there, for the Jewish rites
of purification, each holding twenty or thirty gallons. Jesus said
to them, "Fill the jars with water." And they filled them up to
the brim. He said to them, "Now draw some out, and take it to
the steward of the feast." So they took it. When the steward of
the feast tasted the water now become wine, and did not know
where it came from (though the servants who had drawn the
water knew), the steward of the feast called the bridegroom and
said to him, "Every man serves the good wine first; and when
men have drunk freely, then the poor wine; but you have kept
the good wine until now." This, the first of his signs, Jesus did

Total Consecration

at Cana in Galilee, and manifested his glory; and his disciples believed in him.

Meditate on Mary's Intercession with Jesus

Jesus has been with Saint Joseph and Mary in His private life, the family life, for many years. At thirty, Jesus leaves His home to enter into His public ministry. One of His first appearances is in Cana of Galilee at a wedding feast. Mary and some of the Apostles are also present. In the midst of the celebration a serious problem surfaces that could have caused serious embarrassment to the wedding couple—the wine runs out. This problem is noticed by our Lady immediately. She recognizes the intense suffering and embarrassment that could visit this couple, and she comes to the rescue in a way that nobody else would have ever imagined. She gently turns to Jesus and tells Him that there is no more wine. Mary always turns to Jesus, and she wants us always to turn to Him in all that occurs in our lives. As Jesus was the center of Mary's life, so should He be the center of ours!

Consider thoughtfully

Mary's Advice to All
Love and devotion to our Lady must never detract from a deeper love and devotion to Jesus. Just the contrary: our Lady always points us to Jesus and helps us to know and love Him all the more fervently. Remember: she is the quickest, easiest, smoothest, and most efficacious pathway to Jesus. Her words to the servants say it all: "Do whatever He tells you." This is the best advice in the

world! If we would only put into practice these last words of our Lady recorded in the Bible, we would be on the highway to holiness—and to heaven.

Do this now: Holiness and future heavenly glory depend on obeying the Word of God, which Mary commanded the waiters to do at the wedding in Cana. Resolve now that you will listen closely to hear the Word of God, and that when you hear it, you, too, will do whatever He tells you.

The First Miracle of Jesus

When the waiters obeyed Mary and Jesus, Jesus performed His first public miracle, turning water into wine. This miracle confirmed the Apostles in their belief in the person and mission of Jesus, preparing them for their own later mission of bringing Jesus to the whole world. This is one of the many reasons why our Lady is known as Queen of the Apostles.

Do this now: Strive ever to remember the circumstances of this first public miracle of Jesus and, as your consecration approaches, let its message prepare you better for your own coming apostolate.

Go to Mary with Your Problems

No one is free of crosses, temptations, doubt, confusion, fear, and anxiety. In all of the waves that beat against the rudder of your ship, which is the soul God has given you, seek refuge with our Lady. As she so gently but powerfully interceded for the wedding couple, thereby moving Jesus to solve the problem, so she earnestly desires to intervene in your life and to intercede for you before the presence of Jesus, who can do all things. As the angel said in the Annunciation: "For with God nothing will be impossible" (Luke 1:37). Equally true, nothing is impossible for those who turn to our Lady with their problems.

Do this now: Turn to our Lady with a problem and ask her to intercede for you and to help you to do whatever Jesus tells you—that is, whatever action He inspires you to take.

Our Lady Will Lift You Up

In *The Passion of the Christ*, as Jesus carries the heavy cross weighed down by the sins of all of humanity, including your sins and mine, there is a short flashback. It shows Jesus as a little boy falling. Our Lady leaves all and rushes to lift Him up. In the same way she wants to rush to you and lift you up. Our Lady is quick to sense our moments of difficulty and to rush to our aid! As we pray in the Memorare: "Never was it known that anyone who fled to thy protection, implored thy help, or sought thine intercession was left unaided."

Do this now: When you probe the depths of your heart, you may discover there a thorn of sorrow, a serious problem gnawing away at you and taking away your peace. Open your heart to Mary right now and talk to her about this problem. Our Lady listened attentively to the angel; she listened attentively to Saint Joseph; she listened attentively to Jesus. Our Lady is the best of listeners. Right now, tell her what is weighing you down, what is heavy on your heart. She is there to help you.

Cana and Your Consecration

The presence of our Lady at Cana and her power of intercession is a very important passage for your consecration to Jesus through Mary. Why? Because you want to give all that you have and are to Jesus through Mary. Through her prayers, our Lady will turn your water into wine. As Jesus worked miracles in His life, and the first was turning water into wine through our Lady's intercession, so He can work tremendous miracles in your life if you entrust your whole life into the hands and heart of Mary.

Do this now: Share all your problems with Mary. Do you have family problems? Bring them to our Lady, and she will help. Money problems? She can help you and your family if you do all you can and trust. Problems with your spouse or a loved one? Our Lady is near; call upon her holy name. Rebellious children? Lift your heart to Mary, and she can obtain very special graces. Failing health? Turn to our Lady, Health of the Sick. Dryness or darkness or aridity in prayer? Turn to our Lady, and she will help you to be faithful in prayer; the clouds will dissipate; the noonday sun will shine again. Do temptations assault you day and night? Turn to our Lady, and she will crush the ugly head of the ancient serpent.

Your Consecration Approaches

Your consecration is close at hand. Consider the promises involved in it. You belong to Jesus through the intercession of Mary. Give her all you have, and she will give you the greatest gift: Jesus!

Do this now: On the next page, you will find the Consecration Prayer that you will pray and sign once you are ready to give yourself completely to Jesus through Mary. Pray it now with all your heart, slowly, calmly, and with the greatest confidence and trust in Mary's powerful intercession in the presence of Jesus. Don't make the consecration yet, and don't sign it. That will come later. Rather, from this day forward keep in mind the promises in the prayer and strive to live in accordance with them until the day, not long from now, when you will make your final consecration by signing the Consecration Prayer.

Preview of your act of consecration

O eternal and incarnate Wisdom! O sweetest and most adorable Jesus! True God and true man, only Son of the Eternal Father, and of Mary, always virgin! I adore Thee profoundly in the bosom and splendors of Thy Father during eternity; and I adore Thee also in the virginal womb of Mary, Thy most worthy Mother, in the time of Thine Incarnation.

I give Thee thanks that Thou hast annihilated Thyself, taking the form of a slave in order to rescue me from the cruel slavery of the devil. I praise and glorify Thee that Thou hast been pleased to submit Thyself to Mary, Thy holy Mother, in all things, in order to make me Thy faithful slave through her.

But, alas! ungrateful and faithless as I have been, I have not kept the promises that I made so solemnly to Thee in my Baptism; I have not fulfilled my obligations; I do not deserve to be called Thy child, nor yet Thy slave. And as there is nothing in me that does not merit Thine anger and Thy repulse, I dare not come by myself before Thy most holy and august majesty. It is on this account that I have recourse to the intercession of Thy most holy Mother, whom Thou hast given me for a mediatrix with Thee. It is through her that I hope to obtain of Thee contrition, the pardon of my sins, and the acquisition and preservation of wisdom.

Hail, then, O immaculate Mary, living tabernacle of the Divinity, where the Eternal Wisdom willed to be hidden and to be adored by angels and by men! Hail, O Queen of Heaven and Earth, to whose empire everything that is under God is subject. Hail, O sure refuge of sinners, whose mercy fails no one. Hear my desires for Divine Wisdom; and for that end receive the vows and offerings that in my lowliness I present to thee.

I, _____, a faithless sinner, renew and ratify today in thy hands the vows of my Baptism; I renounce forever Satan, his pomps, and his works; and I give myself entirely to Jesus Christ, the Incarnate Wisdom, to carry my cross after Him all the days of my life, and to be more faithful to Him than I have ever been before.

In the presence of all the heavenly court, I choose thee this day for my Mother and Mistress. I deliver and consecrate to thee, as thy slave, my body and soul, my goods, both interior and exterior, and even the value of all my good actions, past, present, and future; leaving to thee the entire and full right of disposing of me, and all that belongs to me, without exception, according to thy good pleasure, for the greater glory of God in time and in eternity.

Receive, O benignant Virgin, this little offering of my slavery, in honor of, and in union with, that subjection that the Eternal Wisdom deigned to have to thy maternity; in homage to the power that both of you have over this poor sinner; and in thanksgiving for the privileges with which the Holy Trinity has favored thee. I declare that I wish henceforth, as thy true slave, to seek thy honor and to obey thee in all things.

O admirable Mother, present me to thy dear Son as His eternal slave, so that, as He has redeemed me by thee, by thee He may receive me!

O Mother of mercy, grant me the grace to obtain the true Wisdom of God; and for that end receive me among those whom thou lovest and teachest, whom thou leadest, nourishest, and protectest as thy children and thy slaves.

O faithful Virgin, make me in all things so perfect a disciple, imitator, and slave of the Incarnate Wisdom, Jesus Christ, thy Son, that I may attain, by thine intercession and by thine example, to the fullness of His age on earth and of His glory in Heaven. Amen.

Signature: _____

Date: _____

Day 7

REPETITION

Repeat one of the mysteries on which you meditated this week. You might choose a meditation during which God moved you and poured abundant consolations into your soul. There may be more consolations waiting for you. Like a bee that returns to a flower for more nectar, return to the flower of this meditation for more spiritual nectar.

St. Ignatius suggests that sometimes it's good to choose a meditation during which you experienced desolation. Why? Desolation in prayer often manifests a certain resistance on our part to grace. Ask the Holy Spirit to help you break down that resistance through repetition.

Enter into the meditation, beginning with the steps found on pages 10 and 11.

Week 5

The Seven Sorrows of the Virgin Mary

Day 1: First Sorrow of Mary

THE PROPHECY OF SIMEON

Luke 2:22–35
Read slowly and prayerfully

And when the time came for their purification according to the law of Moses, they brought him up to Jerusalem to present him to the Lord (as it is written in the law of the Lord, "Every male that opens the womb shall be called holy to the Lord") and to offer a sacrifice according to what is said in the law of the Lord, "a pair of turtledoves, or two young pigeons."

Now there was a man in Jerusalem, whose name was Simeon, and this man was righteous and devout, looking for the consolation of Israel, and the Holy Spirit was upon him. And it had been revealed to him by the Holy Spirit that he should not see death before he had seen the Lord's Christ. And inspired by the Spirit he came into the temple; and when the parents brought in the child Jesus, to do for him according to the custom of the law, he took him up in his arms and blessed God and said,

"Lord, now lettest thou thy servant depart in peace,
according to thy word;
for mine eyes have seen thy salvation

which thou hast prepared in the presence of all peoples,
a light for revelation to the Gentiles,
and for glory to thy people Israel."

And his father and his mother marveled at what was said
about him; and Simeon blessed them and said to Mary his
mother,

"Behold, this child is set for the fall and rising of many
     in Israel,
and for a sign that is spoken against
(and a sword will pierce through your own soul also),
that thoughts out of many hearts may be revealed."

Meditate on the sword that pierces Mary's heart

The huge sword in this prophecy would indeed pierce the heart
of Mary, especially thirty-three years later, during the Passion,
Crucifixion, and death of our Lord and Savior, Jesus Christ.
Nonetheless, our Lady willingly accepts God's will in its fullness and conforms her heart and will to it. In this, she teaches
us a most valuable lesson: holiness and interior peace of heart,
mind, and soul depend on discerning the will of God, accepting
it, and striving to put it into practice in our daily lives. As you
head toward your consecration to Jesus through Mary, enter into
your heart, see the swords of sorrow that have pierced it, and
bring these to our Lady in prayer. Have no fear! Open your heart
totally to your Heavenly Mother, who loves you so much. She
desires that you have a total trust in her as well as in her Son,
Jesus. "Jesus and Mary, I trust in you!"

Consider thoughtfully

Mary Stayed Close to Jesus

In the midst of the sorrows of life, we must learn from Mary this very simple but profound lesson: stay close to Jesus; cling to Him and never detach yourself from Him!

Do this now: Mary actually held the Baby Jesus in her arms. In your sorrows, imitate the Infant Jesus and find refuge in the arms of Mary.

Obedience Is Almost Always Difficult

Mary and Saint Joseph obey the Mosaic Law and present Jesus in the Temple. One of the most challenging struggles we might experience is that of obedience. God calls us to obey the Church, obey the Commandments, obey our confessor, obey our state of life, and obey a well-formed conscience, but all too often we run in the wrong direction, and this causes us great interior conflict and suffering.

Do this now: Pray that you can learn from Jesus, Mary, and Saint Joseph that true freedom can be discovered in obedience to lawful authority. Likely, many of your past sorrows came because of disobedience. Enter into conversation with Mary, and talk to her about obedience; ask her for advice and counsel on how to improve in this all-important virtue.

Mary's Role as Co-Redemptrix

Our Lady's yes to the angel was also a yes to her future collaboration in the work of salvation with Jesus. For this reason, one of the sublime modern titles of Mary is "Co-Redemptrix."

This title is used in the documents of Vatican II, which state that our Lady collaborated with Jesus in the salvation and redemption of the world. This would be true especially as Jesus hung on the Cross and Our Lady, "*Stabat Mater*," stood at the foot of the Cross. Jesus offered Himself for the salvation of the world. Our Lady in her Sorrowful and Immaculate Heart also offered her beloved Son to the Eternal Father for the salvation of the world.

Do this now: The two Hearts of Jesus and Mary were intimately united at all times. Enter now into dialogue with Mary about Jesus and His love for you. Ask Our Lady of Sorrows to soften your heart, to make you docile and open to God's heavenly inspirations, like the dewfall on the morning grass!

Simeon's Words of Dismissal

"Lord, now lettest thou thy servant depart in peace,... for mine eyes have seen thy salvation." Nuns, brothers, and priests throughout the world recall Simeon's words in Compline, the prayer that concludes the day. These words refer to the end of our life. As we are dying we want Jesus, Mary, and Saint Joseph to be with us to accompany us from this life to the next.

Do this now: Turn now to Our Lady of Sorrows and with all the fervor in your heart beg her for the grace of all graces — the grace of a holy and happy death. Ask that in the midst of the tempests and turmoil of life you will be found faithful to the end. May the Hail Mary, especially its conclusion, be your prayer of dismissal from this life to the next: "Holy Mary, Mother of God, pray for us sinners now and at the hour of our death. Amen."

Finally, carry your crosses with Jesus

In *The Imitation of Christ*, Thomas à Kempis says that the life of Jesus from the crib to the grave was a cross. It was through a willing acceptance of the Cross that Jesus, Son of Mary and Son of the Eternal Father, redeemed the world. For this reason Saint Francis prayed: "We adore you, O Christ, and we praise you because by your holy Cross you have redeemed the world." Memorize this brief prayer, and pray it silently but fervently many times as you go about your daily tasks.

Day 2: Second Sorrow of Mary

THE FLIGHT INTO EGYPT

Matthew 2:7–23
Read slowly and prayerfully

Then Herod summoned the wise men secretly and ascertained from them what time the star appeared; and he sent them to Bethlehem, saying, "Go and search diligently for the child, and when you have found him bring me word, that I too may come and worship him." When they had heard the king they went their way; and lo, the star which they had seen in the East went before them, till it came to rest over the place where the child was. When they saw the star, they rejoiced exceedingly with great joy; and going into the house they saw the child with Mary his mother, and they fell down and worshiped him. Then, opening their treasures, they offered him gifts, gold and frankincense and myrrh. And being warned in a dream not to return to Herod, they departed to their own country by another way.

Now when they had departed, behold, an angel of the Lord appeared to Joseph in a dream and said, "Rise, take the child and his mother, and flee to Egypt, and remain there till I tell you; for Herod is about to search for the child, to destroy him." And he rose and took the child and his mother by night, and departed to Egypt, and remained there until the death of Herod. This was to fulfil what the Lord had spoken by the prophet, "Out of Egypt have I called my son."

Then Herod, when he saw that he had been tricked by the wise men, was in a furious rage, and he sent and killed all the male children in Bethlehem and in all that region who were two years old or under, according to the time which he had ascertained from the wise men. Then was fulfilled what was spoken by the prophet Jeremiah:

"A voice was heard in Ramah,
wailing and loud lamentation,
Rachel weeping for her children;
she refused to be consoled,
because they were no more."

But when Herod died, behold, an angel of the Lord appeared in a dream to Joseph in Egypt, saying, "Rise, take the child and his mother, and go to the land of Israel, for those who sought the child's life are dead." And he rose and took the child and his mother, and went to the land of Israel. But when he heard that Archelaus reigned over Judea in place of his father Herod, he was afraid to go there, and being warned in a dream he withdrew to the district of Galilee. And he went and dwelt in a city called Nazareth, that what was spoken by the prophets might be fulfilled, "He shall be called a Nazarene."

Meditate on Saint Joseph

True devotion and love for Mary cannot be separated from real knowledge of and devotion to Saint Joseph, the husband of Mary. Joseph was the provider, protector, and support of the Holy

Family. In the dangers that you experience in life, you should also turn with confidence to Saint Joseph, and he will most certainly come to your aid.

Consider thoughtfully

The Joseph in Genesis
In Genesis, we read about another Joseph, who is one of the most noble personalities in the entire Bible. Despite sufferings, persecutions, temptations, and trials, he focused always on doing God's will rather than on pleasing men. Consequently, God raised him to one of the highest positions in the kingdom of Egypt — chief administrator of food during a worldwide famine. In this time of famine, "Go to Egypt, go to Joseph" was the only hope for many, including Joseph's brothers in the land of Canaan, who, out of jealousy and envy, had sold Joseph to traders when he was only a boy, telling their father that a wild animal had killed their younger brother.

Do this now: We are called to go to Joseph, the husband of Mary and the foster father of Jesus. Turn to him now; he is there to help you at all times and in all places. Simply call upon him.

Bloody King Herod
Imagine this horrendous scene! The Magi take another route to return to their country and so avoid meeting up again with King Herod. Furious, this wicked, insecure, bloodthirsty king issues a decree to kill all the boys in Bethlehem and its vicinity who are two years and under so as to secure his kingdom and authority. The child targeted is Jesus, the Son of Mary! Jesus is

the archenemy of King Herod. There cannot be two kings at the same time; one of these has to die, and that is Jesus. That is the mindset of King Herod.

Do this now: In less dramatic but just as serious ways, you, too, are faced with a choice of rulers. Who will be your king: Jesus or worldly values? Pray that Jesus will give you the grace always to choose to serve Him, lest you choose the world and die spiritually.

God Has His Plans

God sends an angel to warn Saint Joseph in a dream that fleeing from the wicked king is the only route to salvation. Without any hesitation, good Saint Joseph prepares Jesus and Mary for the long, perilous flight that will terminate in Egypt.

Do this now: Ask Saint Joseph that, like him, you will be open and ready to follow the good inspirations that God sends you.

Titles of Saint Joseph

Good Saint Joseph was very important for Jesus and Mary; therefore, he should be important for you, too! Saint Joseph has many titles: Master of the Interior Life, Model of Workers, Ornament of the Domestic Life, Patron of Fathers, Patron of Husbands, Patron of Families, Terror of Demons, Patron of the Universal Church, Patron of Purity, and Patron of a Holy and Happy Death.

Do this now: As you continue on your journey toward the day of your consecration to Jesus through Mary, invite Saint Joseph into your consecration. Read through these many beautiful titles in honor of him and pray over them; allow them to sink deeply into your heart. May they instill in you a great trust and confidence in Saint Joseph, husband of Mary.

Travel with Saint Joseph

Contemplate this painful but consoling scene: Joseph taking Mary and the Child Jesus and leading them from danger to safety. Traveling from Nazareth to Egypt was no easy task. It was a lengthy, tiring trip. No restaurants, motels, resorts, or vacation stops along the way! During the day, the scathing sun could have easily burned them as they traveled through the desert. Nights, quite the contrary, they must have experienced bitter cold. It was the warmth of their love for each other that kept them warm—the fire of the love of the Holy Spirit.

Do this now: Imagine that you are traveling with the Holy Family. Contemplate them! Your consecration consists in establishing a constant conversation with our Lady, with Jesus, and with Saint Joseph. Open up and talk to them; they are very interested in you and what is going on in your life's journey, the difficulties you have known or may be facing right now.

Consider God's Presence in Your Life

Right now you are still on a journey, just as Saint Joseph was as he led, fed, protected, and supported Jesus and Mary. Among the many sublime virtues of good Saint Joseph are those of being a provider and a protector. As head of the Holy Family, he provided for their needs—both material and spiritual. Furthermore, he protected Jesus and Mary from the dangers that surrounded them—in this case, the evil intention of King Herod to kill Jesus.

Do this now: Enter into deep conversation with good Saint Joseph about your journey through life. To facilitate it, rewind the film of your life; ask for the grace to see God's providential hand in all the moments of your life: your childhood years and God's presence; your adolescent years and God's loving and providential presence; your early adult years and God walking with you, protecting you, inviting you back to Him, always gently, always respecting your freedom. All in all, God has never been distant from you, although you may have distanced yourself from Him. Review your life and talk to Saint Joseph about it all.

Face Dangers with Saint Joseph's Help

Today more than ever we are surrounded by so many dangers—physical, economic, psychological, moral, and spiritual. We might even use the image of being surrounded by a pack of dangerous and ravenous wolves. Saint Joseph can provide for us and protect us. He is just as strong now as he was two thousand years ago. In your prayers, bring these dangers to both Joseph and Mary, and they will bring them to the Heart of Jesus.

Do this now: Implore Saint Joseph to be your protector against present dangers. Pray: "From the wolf of pornography, Saint Joseph, save me and my family. From the fierce wolf of abortion, killing innocent babies like Herod, Saint Joseph, save my family and all innocent babies! Because of the legalization of same-sex unions, an attack against the very core and center of the family, good Saint Joseph, patron of the family, come to the rescue of my family and all families! Because of the constant threat of ISIS and other militant groups that, like Herod, are out to destroy lives, Saint Joseph, pray for me and my family and please protect us. Because of the constant danger of materialism, sensuality, and hedonism—the philosophy of pleasure as god — good Saint Joseph, pray for me and help me to focus on Jesus, Mary, and your loving presence as my true and lasting haven and refuge! Good Saint Joseph, in all of my dangers, present and future, I entrust myself and my family to you, as Mary and God the Father entrusted the Baby Jesus to you."

Finally, always stay close to Joseph

Consecration to our Lady must include the ones whom Mary loved most, as well as the ones who loved Mary most. Of course, aside from Jesus, Saint Joseph was the one who loved Mary most! Our lives have many dangers from within and from without. God has entrusted Mary and Saint Joseph to you as your close guardians to help you journey through life and make it safely to heaven. Right now, place the rest of your journey in life in the hands of glorious Saint Joseph. End your meditation with a triple conversation: one with Saint Joseph, another with the Blessed Virgin Mary, and finally a long conversation with the Lord Jesus Christ.

Day 3: Third Sorrow of Mary

JESUS LOST FOR THREE DAYS

Luke 2:41–52
Read slowly and prayerfully

Now his parents went to Jerusalem every year at the feast of the
Passover. And when he was twelve years old, they went up according to custom; and when the feast was ended, as they were
returning, the boy Jesus stayed behind in Jerusalem. His parents
did not know it, but supposing him to be in the company they
went a day's journey, and they sought him among their kinsfolk
and acquaintances; and when they did not find him, they returned to Jerusalem, seeking him. After three days they found
him in the temple, sitting among the teachers, listening to them
and asking them questions; and all who heard him were amazed
at his understanding and his answers. And when they saw him
they were astonished; and his mother said to him, "Son, why
have you treated us so? Behold, your father and I have been
looking for you anxiously." And he said to them, "How is it that
you sought me? Did you not know that I must be in my Father's
house?" And they did not understand the saying which he spoke
to them. And he went down with them and came to Nazareth,

and was obedient to them; and his mother kept all these things in her heart.

And Jesus increased in wisdom and in stature, and in favor with God and man.

Meditate on losing the Child Jesus

The third sorrow of Mary and the Fifth Joyful Mystery of the Holy Rosary both concern the loss of the Child Jesus in the Temple. There is a blending of joy and sorrow. This is a foreshadowing of Jesus' being lost for three days by being buried in the tomb and then being found in His glorious Resurrection on Easter Sunday. Let us meditate upon this sorrow of Mary with great openness of heart and beg to share, at least to a limited degree, in the sufferings of the Sorrowful and Immaculate Heart of Mary.

Consider thoughtfully

They Traveled Joyfully Together

Imagine that you are traveling to Jerusalem with the Holy Family. Being united with each other brings joy to their faces. They truly enjoy each other and enjoy your company, too. As you admire the three holiest and humblest persons in the world, you will be moved to talk with them.

Do this now: Enter into conversation with good Saint Joseph; tell him what is on your mind. Then talk to Our Lady about what is in your heart. Then talk to Jesus about your life and what is going on in your heart. Then you can talk to all three of them at the same time. They are the best of listeners as you talk to them individually, as well as collectively. They rejoice in your presence, your friendship, and your conversation.

They Lose Jesus

After the Holy Family's pilgrimage to Jerusalem, they start their trip home to Nazareth. It was the custom of the Jewish people for women to travel in one group and men in another and then meet up at the end of the day. After a day's journey Saint Joseph and Mary discover, to their great sorrow, that Jesus, the greatest treasure of their life, is with neither of them nor with relatives. He is lost—totally lost—and they do not know where He is!

Do this now: In your prayer as you prepare yourself for your total consecration to Jesus through Mary, strive to enter into the Sorrowful and the Immaculate Heart of Mary now in the midst of this terrible affliction—Mary has lost her only Son! Another one of the swords that the prophet Simeon has foretold pierces her tender and loving mother's heart. Be with Mary in her immense sorrow and talk to her; try to do all you possibly can to console her and help her in her pursuit of Jesus.

The Loss of a Child

Perhaps, although you are a loving mother, you have sometimes lost one of your children or maybe more than one. Call to mind when you lost your little one at the mall; he was lost and you could not find him. Finally, after five minutes, from behind some pile of merchandise he appears with tears in his eyes. He spots you and runs with all the energy in his little body to throw himself into your arms. He weeps, and you weep—tears of immense sorrow, but also tears of great joy upon the encounter and embrace!

Mary did not lose her Child Jesus for five minutes in a shopping mall or a supermarket, as most likely was your case. On the contrary, Mary lost Jesus for three long days in the enormous city of Jerusalem, in the midst of thousands of travelers.

Do this now: Be with Mary these three long days that seem never to end. Be with her as she inquires among relatives and friends whether they know where Jesus is or have seen Him. All respond in the negative: "We don't know where Jesus is." Our Lady's pain and sorrow increase. Be with her in her sorrow to console her. Talk to her about Jesus and your willingness to search with her for Jesus until He is found! Indeed, you are called to be a ray of hope, a note of joy, a dawn rising in Mary's intense sorrow. Our Lady truly appreciates your presence, your conversation, your words of comfort, and your willingness to suffer with her the loss of Jesus. Your relationship with her is growing stronger as you pass from one mystery in her life to another. Your consecration will result in your giving of your total being to Mary in total trust. In the journey through your life, beg Jesus, Mary, and Saint Joseph to be your constant companions.

They Find Jesus in the Temple

Finally after three days of searching, our Lady and Saint Joseph return to the Temple of Jerusalem, and to their immense joy there is Jesus in the midst of the doctors of the Law, the students and teachers of the Bible. What is He doing? He is attentively listening to them, asking them questions, and—this is of great importance—teaching them even though He is only twelve years of age! Already we perceive one of the primary roles that Jesus would carry out starting at thirty years of age—the role of Teacher, the greatest Teacher who ever existed! The doctors of the Law are fascinated. Never have they met a child as intelligent, wise, and brilliant as this prodigy.

Do this now: Ask Joseph and Mary to help you learn to imitate the Child Jesus in the Temple by listening to them as they speak to you, by asking questions so that you may come to know them better, and by teaching those for whom you are spiritually responsible, particularly your own children.

Mary's Question to Jesus

Upon finding Jesus, Mary responds: "Son, why have you treated us so? Behold, your father and I have been looking for you anxiously." Jesus gives a mysterious response: "How is it that you sought me? Did you not know that I must be in my Father's house?" Neither Saint Joseph nor Mary understand His words. Then Jesus returns with them to Nazareth, and He grows in wisdom and age and grace before God and man.

Do this now: Meditate upon these powerful lessons and talk to our Lady about them; draw closer and closer to her because she loves you and has a special place for you in her heart. Seek to develop a constant union with her Immaculate Heart and with Jesus, whom she wants to enthrone as the king of your life.

Ask Mary to Help You with Your Losses

Mary lost Jesus and searched for Him. As you grow in knowledge of Mary and love for her, you will long ever more intensely to share your sufferings and losses with her.

Do this now: Have you lost a loved one through death? Talk to Mary about this sorrow. Have you lost a son who has given himself over to vices—drinking or drugs or immorality? Speak to our Lady about this thorn that pierces your heart. Have you lost a daughter who has decided to live in an immoral relationship? Tell our Lady how you feel about this apparent betrayal.

The Spiritual Loss of Family Members

Perhaps even more painful is the spiritual loss of loved ones. Possibly right now you are suffering because some of those persons you love most have abandoned their love for Jesus, Mary, and Saint Joseph. Still more, they have abandoned the Church and the practice of the sacraments. This reality pierces and penetrates your heart. Our Lady's loss of Jesus and her intense suffering is related to the moral and spiritual loss of your loved ones.

Do this now: Open up your wounded heart and talk to our Lady, Mother of consolation, about the spiritual loss of your children, or your spouse, or another loved one. Our Lady longs to listen to you; she will understand you and will comfort you most dearly.

The Mysteries in Your Life

Even after finding Jesus in the Temple after three days of sorrowful searching, Mary did not understand her beloved Son's explanation telling why He was there. In your life, there are sufferings that you possibly do not fully comprehend. They are puzzles or enigmas to you. Sometimes life itself does not seem to make sense.

Do this now: Open your heart to our Lady and tell her your sorrows and the painful mysteries in your life that don't seem to make sense. She will help you to understand what can be understood and to bear graciously what cannot.

Finally, consider the effects of mortal sin

If you ever have the misfortune of losing Jesus in the Temple of your heart because you've committed a mortal sin, never give in to despair. On the contrary, trust all the more in the powerful intercession of our Lady, Refuge of Sinners. Return to the loving embrace of the Father (see the parable of the prodigal son: Luke 15:11–32). Turn to our Lady and beg for the grace to make the best sacramental Confession in your life and return to a more fervent love for Jesus. Ask our Lady to help you to live in grace, but if you fall, return to the Lord with true sorrow and a firm purpose of amendment, trusting that your love for Jesus will become even more intense. May Mary, Refuge of Sinners and Mother of Mercy, be with you, to accompany you all the days of your life until you arrive safely to the port of Heaven!

Day 4: Fourth Sorrow of Mary

THE WAY OF THE CROSS

Luke 23:26–27
Read slowly and prayerfully

And as they led him away, they seized one Simon of Cyrene, who was coming in from the country, and laid on him the cross, to carry it behind Jesus. And there followed him a great multitude of the people, and of women who bewailed and lamented him.

Meditate on the Way of the Cross

To enter into the depths of the love of Jesus and Mary for us, we should cultivate the habit of making the Way of the Cross. These fourteen stations are moments in the Passion, suffering, and death of Jesus. Our Lady was present with Jesus in His bitter agony, Passion, and death. You are called to be with her, to share with her the sufferings of Jesus.

Consider thoughtfully

Go with Jesus and Mary
To help you plumb the depths of the suffering of Jesus that our Lady willingly shared with Him, view the film *The Passion of the Christ*. This film depicts in a masterly manner Mary's presence and following of Jesus. Like Mary we should long to be with Jesus in these last critical moments of His life. Try to view the film not simply as a Hollywood rendition, but as a contemplative prayer. Like Mary Magdalene, be with our Lady every step along the way. As Jesus climbed Calvary, where He would be nailed to the Cross for our eternal salvation, Our Lady walked with Him, contemplated Him, and held Jesus in the depths of her Sorrowful and Immaculate Heart. On the other side was Satan with an ugly little child in his arms looking gleefully and sadistically at Jesus in His suffering. Our life will be marked with lights and consolations, but also moments of temptation and darkness. We should stay close to Mary at all times, but especially in our dark moments and moments of temptation.

> *Do this now*: Talk to Mary about your trials, temptations, crosses, dark moments, and even your doubts. Our Lady understands you and can help you, but you must turn to her with limitless trust. She desires most ardently for you to open up your heart and confide in her. Her prayers are powerful, and she is gently and patiently waiting for you to call out to her.

Our Lady Meets Jesus Bearing the Cross
Try to enter with your imagination into this encounter between Jesus, the Man of Sorrows, and Our Lady of Sorrows. Try now

to see Jesus through the eyes and the Heart of Mary. He is exhausted! The crown of thorns hangs on His bloodstained brow. His face is caked with blood, the Precious Blood that Mary gave to Him in His humanity. His back, side, and stomach are almost an open wound from the scourging that occurred just a few hours earlier. Jesus suffered the scourging at the pillar as a result of our sins of impurity. When He reaches the top of Calvary, His garments will be roughly ripped from His body, causing fresh blood to flow. Even though Jesus is suffering intensely as He climbs Calvary, this encounter with His Mother offers Him consolation. In the midst of His horrible sufferings and those that are about to fall upon Him, His Mother's great love and compassion for Him encourages and strengthens Him.

Do this now: Be with Our Lady as she contemplates the sweating and bloody face of Jesus. Console Jesus with your words, your intentions, and your heart full of love and compassion.

Our Lady of Fatima and Purity

Our Lady of Fatima warned that most souls are lost for all eternity due to the sins against the virtue of purity. Turn to our Lady as she contemplates the suffering Jesus, her Lord, God, and Son, and beseech her for the precious virtue of purity. "Blessed are the pure in heart, for they shall see God" (Matt. 5:8). Purity is the virtue of the strong.

Do this now: Beg our Lady to pray for you so as to purify your memory of bad images. Invoke her for the grace to be able to focus your eyes on Jesus and avoid any glances or looks that can jeopardize the virtue of purity. Implore our Lady to intercede for you so that you will not give in to abusing your eyes by fixing your attention on any images that would hurt the Hearts of Jesus and Mary. Call out to Mary and beg her to watch over your social relations so that you will avoid associating with and connecting emotionally with any persons who could place in danger your virtue of purity. If you are married, beg for the grace to live a more innocent, pure, chaste, and noble relationship with your spouse. Ask our Lady to pray that you will never allow yourself to be used as an object or ever use another person as an object.

Your Body Is a Temple of the Holy Spirit

You were created in the image and likeness of God. Through holy Baptism you became a son or daughter of God. Our Lady will teach you the importance of purity related to your innate dignity. Still more, through her powerful prayers, she will remind you of your destiny. Your body is indeed the temple of the Holy Spirit. Your destiny is to be with Jesus and Mary, the angels, and the saints for all eternity in heaven. This, of course, entails turning to our Lady and begging for purity and holiness, and to be filled with true love for God and neighbor.

Do this now: As you prepare for your consecration to our Lady, turn to her now and implore her for the grace of purity of eyes, mind, body, heart, and even intention.

Finally, share your crosses with Mary and Jesus

Once again delve into the depths of your heart, into the nitty gritty of your own life and you will discover a thorn, a splinter, a deep sorrow that maybe up to this point you have not had enough courage to see and admit. Now is the time to recognize and admit your own thorns, splinters, and sorrows. The key to sanctity, peace, and salvation is to bring these to Our Lady. Talk to Our lady about these sufferings right now. Our Lady is the best of listeners and never tires when you, her son/daughter, become vulnerable and reveal your wounds to her. The wounded Jesus looked upon Our Lady; now you with your wounds can look to Our Lady. She will never be deaf to your plea or turn a blind eye to your sufferings. On the contrary, in your sorrow she will rush to your rescue! How blessed we are to be consecrating our whole lives to Our Lady and that includes our own passion, suffering, and dark and lonely nights!

Day 5: Fifth Sorrow of Mary

THE CRUCIFIXION

John 19:16–30
Read slowly and prayerfully

Then he handed him over to them to be crucified.

So they took Jesus, and he went out, bearing his own cross, to the place called the place of a skull, which is called in Hebrew Golgotha. There they crucified him, and with him two others, one on either side, and Jesus between them. Pilate also wrote a title and put it on the cross; it read, "Jesus of Nazareth, the King of the Jews." Many of the Jews read this title, for the place where Jesus was crucified was near the city; and it was written in Hebrew, in Latin, and in Greek. The chief priests of the Jews then said to Pilate, "Do not write, 'The King of the Jews,' but, 'This man said, I am King of the Jews.'" Pilate answered, "What I have written I have written."

When the soldiers had crucified Jesus they took his garments and made four parts, one for each soldier; also his tunic. But the tunic was without seam, woven from top to bottom; so they said to one another, "Let us not tear it, but cast lots for it to see whose it shall be." This was to fulfil the scripture,

"They parted my garments among them,
and for my clothing they cast lots."

So the soldiers did this. But standing by the cross of Jesus were his mother, and his mother's sister, Mary the wife of Clopas, and Mary Magdalene. When Jesus saw his mother, and the disciple whom he loved standing near, he said to his mother, "Woman, behold, your son!" Then he said to the disciple, "Behold, your mother!" And from that hour the disciple took her to his own home.

After this Jesus, knowing that all was now finished, said (to fulfil the scripture), "I thirst." A bowl full of vinegar stood there; so they put a sponge full of the vinegar on hyssop and held it to his mouth. When Jesus had received the vinegar, he said, "It is finished"; and he bowed his head and gave up his spirit.

Meditate on the nailing of Jesus to the Cross

This fifth sorrow of Mary is her witnessing the cruel death of her beloved Son.

Consider thoughtfully

Jesus Is Crucified

Our Lady sees the soldiers roughly throw Jesus' sacred body to the ground. Mary sees them extend Jesus' hand—the hand that He used to bless children and heal the sick—and nail it to the Cross. Blood trickles forth—the Precious Blood that Mary gave to Jesus. Then they extend His other hand and mercilessly pull his shoulder out of joint as Jesus writhes in pain. As our Lady witnesses this, the sword of sorrow pierces her heart. Then they nail the feet of the Man who went about bringing good tidings to the poor, the sick, the abandoned, the lepers, and the rejected of society. The feet whose first steps Mary watched when Jesus was a baby are fastened tightly to the Cross with nails. His Sacred Blood gushes forth to forgive our sins and obtain for us eternal salvation. All this time our Lady watches with her eyes and contemplates in her immaculate and sorrowful heart Jesus' redemptive suffering and death.

Do this now: Thank Mary for giving Jesus His sacred humanity, which He offered as a holocaust for our salvation. Be with our Lady as the Cross is elevated on high and then roughly thrust into the ground, racking Jesus' body with more pain.

Mary Listens to Jesus' Last Words

Our Lady stands beneath the Cross and contemplates Jesus with her eyes and her heart. She listens to the words that Jesus pronounces as, dying on the Cross, He delivers His final and most eloquent sermon. With Mary, we are there to listen to His words attentively.

Do this now: With Mary, listen to the Seven Last Words of Christ:

♦ "Father, forgive them; for they know not what they do." (Luke 23:34)

♦ "I thirst." (John 19:28)

♦ "Woman, behold, your son!... [Son] behold, your Mother!" (John 19:26–27)

♦ "My God, my God, why hast thou forsaken me?" (Matt. 27:46)

- ✦ "Truly, I say to you, today you will be with me in Paradise." (Luke 23:43)

- ✦ "Father, into thy hands I commit my spirit." (Luke 23:46)

- ✦ "It is finished." (John 19:30)

Mary Magdalene Represents Penitence

Venerable Fulton J. Sheen states that beneath the Cross we encounter three ways of life. The first is Saint Mary Magdalene, once a public sinner, from whom Jesus cast out seven devils. She was converted by the love of Jesus and the loving presence of Mary.

Do this now: The Magdalene is symbolic of penitence. Strive to be like her in her repentance, in her tears of sorrow, and in her firm purpose of amendment of life.

Saint John Represents the Priesthood ... and Us

Saint John is the beloved disciple who laid his head on the most Sacred Heart of Jesus at the Last Supper. Saint John represents the priesthood. He also represents all of humanity, because when Jesus gave our Lady as Mother to Saint John, He also gave her to all of humanity and to all of us individually as our universal Mother.

Do this now: John took Mary into his home, but more importantly, he took her into the very depths of his heart. In a similar way, as your consecration draws close, take Mary into your home, but, more importantly, take her into your heart.

Our Lady Represents Innocence

Our Lady was conceived without the stain of Original Sin, and she lived a sinless life, never giving in to even the slightest of sins during the whole course of her earthly life. The poet Wordsworth addressed her as "Woman, above all women glorified, our tainted nature's solitary boast." She represents innocence of life.

Do this now: As you stand with the most pure and innocent sorrowful Mother at the foot of the Cross, honestly beseech her for the grace to recognize your sinfulness and for the grace to renounce all sin in your life. "O Mary conceived without sin, pray for us who have recourse to thee."

Finally, embrace spiritual childhood

You are at the foot of the Cross in the person of the beloved disciple, Saint John. In giving John to Mary and Mary to John, Jesus was giving Mary to you as your spiritual Mother for all eternity. In the midst of today's great sorrows, you are called to rejoice because you are not an orphan and will never be an orphan, because our Lady, the Mother of God, the Mother of the Church, the Mother of all of humanity, is truly your Mother, too! Jesus Himself reminds us: "Unless you turn and become like children, you will never enter the kingdom of heaven" (Matt. 18:3). Imagine yourself as a little child safe in the arms of Mary.

Day 6: Sixth Sorrow of Mary

THE PIERCING OF JESUS' SIDE

John 19:31–37
Read slowly and prayerfully

Since it was the day of Preparation, in order to prevent the bodies from remaining on the cross on the sabbath (for that sabbath was a high day), the Jews asked Pilate that their legs might be broken, and that they might be taken away. So the soldiers came and broke the legs of the first, and of the other who had been crucified with him; but when they came to Jesus and saw that he was already dead, they did not break his legs. But one of the soldiers pierced his side with a spear, and at once there came out blood and water. He who saw it has borne witness—his testimony is true, and he knows that he tells the truth—that you also may believe. For these things took place that the scripture might be fulfilled, "Not a bone of him shall be broken." And again another scripture says, "They shall look on him whom they have pierced."

Meditate on Simeon's prophecy fulfilled

Mary was faithful to Jesus always, up to the last moment of His earthly life. Our Lady, the valiant and faithful servant of the Lord, stood beneath the Cross for three long hours as Jesus suffered to save all of humanity.

Consider thoughtfully

Mary Is the Co-Redemptrix

The name *Jesus*, given to Him through the archangel Gabriel at the Annunciation, means "Savior." He came to save you and me from our sins and to open wide the gates of heaven, to give us life and to give it in abundance. The gates of heaven were closed due to the sin of Adam and Eve, but were opened through Jesus, the second Adam, with the collaboration of Mary, the second Eve. Because Mary plays a key role in the redemption of the human race, she merits the title "Co-Redemptrix." In concrete, this means that Mary is associated intimately in the salvific work of Jesus in the Redemption. Jesus is the only and unique redeemer, but Mary collaborates intimately with Jesus in the Redemption of the world. Mary said yes to God at all times and in all places, even in associating herself with the bitter Passion of Jesus.

Do this now: Open up your heart and allow to flow freely abundant sentiments of gratitude toward Jesus and Mary, His Mother and your Mother, for opening the gates of heaven and saving your soul. You can be saved and go to heaven because of the love and the intense suffering of both Jesus and Mary for you. Allow your heart to overflow with the deepest sentiments of gratitude. Talk often to Mary throughout your day and throughout your life. Beg for the grace to live a holy life, renouncing sin and imitating Jesus and Mary so as to attain eternal life!

Mary's Heart Was Also Pierced

Mary witnessed the death of Jesus on the Cross that Friday that we call holy and was nearby when a soldier thrust his lance into Jesus' side. It passed through Jesus' side and penetrated into His Sacred Heart. Then blood and water gushed forth. Jesus did not feel the pain of the lance, for He had already breathed His last, but Our Lady of Sorrows experienced intense pain penetrating the very depths of her most tender heart and soul. This was the sixth sorrow of Mary, the prophecy of Simeon come true: "Behold, this child is set for the fall and rising of many in Israel, and for a sign that is spoken against and a sword will pierce through your own soul), that thoughts out of many hearts may be revealed" (Luke 2:34–35).

Do this now: Your soul was saved and redeemed by the Precious Blood of Jesus that was given to Him through the consent and person of Mary. Contemplate the pierced and open heart of Jesus; contemplate the suffering in the heart and soul of Mary. Our Lady is called the Queen of Martyrs. Her body was not crucified, but the sword that pierced the Sacred Heart of Jesus pierced her Sorrowful and Immaculate Heart.

Seek Refuge in the Two Hearts

In the midst of the struggles of our daily life, the temptations of the devil that assault us constantly, the flesh that seeks to rebel against the spirit, and the world that tries to lie to us, presenting seductive but sinful fashions, we must seek and find a true refuge. The secure refuges of our heart, mind, and soul must be the Sacred Heart of Jesus and the Sorrowful and Immaculate Heart of Mary. These hearts are harbors of safety, oases of peace, and rock-solid foundations.

Do this now: Lift your gaze and open up your heart to the Hearts of Jesus and Mary. Tell Our Lady, who is your dear Mother, all that is going on in your life; your desires; your dreams and aspirations; your fears, doubts, and insecurities. Unload your sorrows, sufferings, and failures on our Lady. She is the best of listeners. Tell our Lady of your moral struggles, your temptations, and even your sins. She is known as the Refuge of Sinners. Undoubtedly, she will obtain for you special graces of repentance, mercy, and true conversion of heart. She can obtain for you the most signal and special graces to overcome any obstacle, but especially the moral obstacle of sin in your life. Fear not, but trust in the Sorrowful and Immaculate Heart of Mary. She is your safe harbor and most secure refuge!

Mary Carries You to Jesus' Sacred Heart

Mary is the quickest and easiest pathway to the Sacred Heart of Jesus. Prayers to the Immaculate Heart of Mary will often bring you to the most Blessed Sacrament, where the Sacred Heart of Jesus is resting and waiting for you. Two friends want to meet through Mary — you and the Sacred Heart of Jesus.

Do this now: Talk to Jesus, the Son of Mary, as your older Brother and your best Friend. Saint John Paul II stated that the living heartbeat of the Church is the most Blessed Sacrament, where Jesus is truly present in His Body, Blood, Soul, and Divinity.

Finally, receive Communion frequently

Your final step through the intercession of Mary is to be present at Holy Mass, participating fully, consciously, and actively. The high point for you at Holy Mass is to receive Holy Communion — the Body and Blood of Jesus that was given through Mary. There is nothing in the world that brings greater joy to the Sorrowful and Immaculate Heart of Mary than when you approach Jesus in the most Blessed Sacrament and receive Him with lively faith, limitless hope, and burning love. Our Lady most earnestly desires that we receive Jesus into our souls in Holy Communion. If we receive Him frequently, fervently, and with the fire of divine love, He will receive us into Heaven, our eternal home, to be with Him and Mary and the angels and saints for all eternity.

THE BURIAL OF JESUS

John 19:38–42
Read slowly and prayerfully

After this Joseph of Arimathea, who was a disciple of Jesus, but secretly, for fear of the Jews, asked Pilate that he might take away the body of Jesus, and Pilate gave him leave. So he came and took away his body. Nicodemus also, who had at first come to him by night, came bringing a mixture of myrrh and aloes, about a hundred pounds' weight. They took the body of Jesus, and bound it in linen cloths with the spices, as is the burial custom of the Jews. Now in the place where he was crucified there was a garden, and in the garden a new tomb where no one had ever been laid. So because of the Jewish day of Preparation, as the tomb was close at hand, they laid Jesus there.

Meditate on Jesus placed in the tomb

In the seventh sorrow of our Lady, the dead body of Jesus is taken from the loving arms of Mary and placed in the tomb and buried.

There is much to meditate on in this last of our Lady's sorrows. Let us beg for extraordinary graces in this contemplation.

Consider thoughtfully

Our Lady of Sorrows

The depth of the suffering and sorrows of our Lady are incomparable, as profound as the depths of the sea. Present at the Passion of Christ, she witnessed Jesus carrying His heavy Cross, loaded with all the sins of humanity, including yours and mine. Our Lady was there on Mount Calvary when Jesus stretched forth His sacred hands to be nailed to the Cross. She was there when the Cross was lifted on high. During those long, bitter three hours during which Jesus hung on the Cross, our Lady valiantly stood at the foot of the Cross, suffering in the depths of her Immaculate Heart what Jesus suffered in His body. For that reason our Lady is called Queen of Martyrs. She listened attentively to the Seven Last Words that issued forth from the compassionate and loving Heart of Jesus that she formed in her womb thirty-three years earlier. Finally, our Lady hear Him give up His spirit into the hands of His Heavenly Father: "Father, into thy hands I commit my spirit" (Luke 23:46). Then, not long after Jesus died, breathing forth His spirit, our Lady witnessed with her eyes and suffered in her heart another key and deeply symbolic event: the piercing of His Sacred Heart. The soldier, whose name is Longinus, looking up at Jesus, as our Lady, too, looked up at her Son, now dead, thrust the lance into His side. Then blood and water gushed forth—symbolic of the sacramental life of the Church. The water symbolizes Baptism, which washes away Original Sin, and Confession, which purifies our souls of personal sin. The blood symbolizes the greatest of all the sacraments—the Holy Eucharist, which is in fact the Body, Blood, Soul, and Divinity of our Lord and Savior, Jesus Christ.

Do this now: Stop now to meditate upon this brief summary of our Lady's sufferings. Ponder how much she suffered for love of you and me. Ponder what went on in the Sorrowful and Immaculate Heart of Mary. Try to penetrate the depths of the heart, mind, and soul of our Lady. Soon you will be consecrating your whole being to her; you will belong totally to her. Talk to her about yourself and your sorrows. Hold nothing back. Mary is the best and the tenderest Mother, and she loves you and cares for you. Your consecration to our Lady will be one of the greatest gifts that God so willingly offers you.

The Pietà

It was our Lady, the Mother of God, who formed the body of Jesus in her womb and gave birth to the body of Jesus as a baby in Bethlehem. She contemplated Him as a baby. She held Him in her arms and cuddled Him after His birth. She saw Him grow into a man. From His conception to His birth in Bethlehem, in their home in Nazareth, in the carpenter shop in Nazareth, through His three-year public ministry in Galilee leading up to His Passion, suffering, and death, our Lady constantly had the body of Jesus before her eyes or in the depths of her Immaculate Heart.

Do this now: Proceed in your prayerful thoughts to gaze upon our Lady holding the dead body of Jesus in her arms. View this with your contemplative eyes as if it were a holy and sacred movie. See the nails taken from the hands of Jesus and then the nails taken from His feet, so that

His body can be lowered from the Cross. Contemplate the deep wounds in His hands and His feet. These are wounds of love that Jesus suffered for you. How great is the love of Jesus and Mary for you even now! Beg Our Lady to help you to penetrate the depths of this mystery, her seventh sorrow.

Mary Receives the Body of Jesus

With the utmost tenderness and compassion, our Lady receives the dead body of her Son, Jesus. In imitation of her, you are called to receive the Body of Jesus into your heart, mind, and soul every time you receive the most Holy Eucharist. Indeed, our Lady can help you to make better Holy Communions and thereby grow in holiness. May she grant you this special grace!

Do this now: Implore the Sorrowful and Immaculate Heart of Mary for the grace to receive the Body and Blood of Jesus in Holy Communion with an ever better disposition. Ask our Lady that you may come to receive the Body of Jesus with lively faith, unbounded and limitless hope, profound humility, a burning and fiery love, and an ardent hunger and thirst.

The Mangled Body of Jesus

Now our Lady holds tenderly to her Immaculate Heart this same body that she gave to Jesus, but the body has been totally transformed by the wiles and wicked intents of evil men. She holds her lifeless Son to her heart and contemplates it in silence. Most artists have not depicted the reality of what the scourged and crucified body of Jesus was like. The film *The Passion of the Christ* has probably come closest to the reality. Our Lady gently takes off the crown of thorns and contemplates His pierced and wounded brow, which she gently caresses and kisses. His hands and His feet are pierced. She contemplates His gaping wounds from the brutal scourging that took place just a few hours earlier. Almost the whole of His sacred body has been reduced to an open wound.

Do this now: Like our Lady, you are invited to caress and kiss His sacred head, pierced for love of you and me. Once again, remember and pray over this: our Lady gave Jesus, the Son of the living God, His humanity. She gave Jesus His body as well as His Precious Blood that He shed on the Cross for our eternal salvation. Now be with Our Lady of Sorrows as she gently wipes the wounds of Jesus. Contemplate the tears welling up in her eyes. Share your own tears with her. Offer yourself as a servant to her. She is always grateful for even the smallest gesture done out of love. Help your sorrowful and loving Mother to wipe His wounds with a cloth.

His Scourging and Wounds

Contemplate the eyes and the person of Our Lady of Sorrows as she looks at these gaping wounds of Jesus, many of them resulting from the brutal scourging. Our Lady of Fatima sadly stated that most souls are lost for all eternity due to sins against the holy virtue of purity. Once again recall that Jesus underwent the scourging at the pillar due to the uncountable number of sins against purity.

Do this now: Once again give your whole self to Mary as you prepare for your consecration to her. Ask her for purity as you contemplate with her the wounds of Jesus, the blood that He shed so abundantly. Implore our Lady for purity of memory, thoughts, and imagination — the transformation of your mind so that you can put on the mind of Christ. Beg her for purity of eyes, that your eyes will always be used to contemplate the good, the noble, the pure, and that which is worthy of the name Christian, a follower of Jesus and Mary. Beg her for purity of body, as your body is indeed a temple of the Holy Spirit from the moment of Baptism. Live out the words of the Apostle Paul: "Whether you eat or drink, or whatever you do, do all to the glory of God" (1 Cor. 10:31) and "Glorify God in your body" (1 Cor. 6:20). Beg our Lady for purity of intention—that all you do will be done for the honor and glory of God, for the salvation of your immortal soul, for the salvation of the souls of your family and loved ones, and for the salvation of all of humanity.

Finally, console Mary

Be with Mary in this sublime moment of her life, as she contemplates for the last time the dead body of Jesus, covered with wounds that He suffered for love of us, covered with blood that He shed to purify our souls from our many sins and to save and redeem us from the grasp of the devil and the pit of hell. How great is the love of Jesus and Mary for us! How sublime and ineffable! Open your heart in love, thanksgiving, supplication, and adoration to our Lady, who is the Co-Redemptrix of all of humanity. Jesus is the unique and only Savior, but He chose our Lady to collaborate intimately with Him in this highest and most important work in the history of humanity. The love of Jesus and Mary for you should indeed transform you into an ardent apostle of that love. Jesus said that He came to bring fire to the earth and that He is not at peace until that fire be enkindled (Luke 12:49). You are called to receive constantly the fire of love from the hearts of Jesus and Mary and to bring this fire of love to the whole world! Love demands a response of love! This response of love is to be a missionary of the love of Jesus and Mary to the whole world, to the most remote regions of the entire universe. "Go therefore and make disciples of all nations, baptizing them in the name of the Father and of the Son and of the Holy Spirit, teaching them to observe all that I have commanded you; and lo, I am with you always, to the close of the age" (Matt. 28:19–20). Right now, firmly resolve to become a true and ardent missionary of the infinite love of the Hearts of Jesus and Mary. The world is waiting and longing for this love!

Conclusion

THE ABUNDANT FRUIT THAT FLOWS FROM CONSECRATION TO JESUS THROUGH MARY

Saint Louis de Montfort states clearly that the quickest, shortest, and easiest path to Jesus is through Mary. Therefore, by conse-crating yourself to Jesus through Mary, you are really taking the shortcut to God, the shortcut to holiness, the shortcut to heaven!

Jesus says that we can know a tree by its fruit. A bad tree will bring forth bad fruit, just as a good tree will bring forth good fruit (Matt. 7:16–18). Jesus is the fruit of the womb of Mary. Saint Louis de Montfort insists that we are called to enter into the womb of Mary; just as she formed Jesus, so Mary also wants to form you into another Jesus. The great Apostle Saint Paul enunciates this truth: "It is no longer I who live, but Christ who lives in me" (Gal. 2:20). Indeed, by consecrating yourself to Jesus through Mary, you can start to imitate Jesus all the more perfectly and radiate His holi-ness: "Be holy as your heavenly Father is holy" (cf. Matt. 5:48).

Before consecrating yourself to Jesus through Mary, on the following pages consider one last time the fruits of this conse-cration, which are abundant: "O taste and see that the LORD is good" (Ps. 34:8). Taste and see and experience the sweetness of the Lord through knowledge and love of His Mother, Mary.

"Hail, Holy Queen, Mother of mercy, our life, our sweetness and our hope!"

Consider thoughtfully

The Riches of the Word of God

Jesus warns us: "Man shall not live by bread alone, but by every word that proceeds from the mouth of God" (Matt. 4:4). Our Lady meditated upon the word of God in her heart. Through your daily meditations on the Word of God, you have come to know Jesus and Mary better, and have come to love them more.

The Gospel Message

The essence of these Marian meditations comes from the Gospel, the Good News of Jesus Christ. Through these meditations, you are yourself becoming a living gospel—good news of joy to the whole world.

Prayer Growth

Your goodwill, time, and efforts spent on these meditations have helped develop your prayer life. What air is to your lungs, so prayer is to your soul—your life's breath! You please Jesus and our Lady with your deeper and more constant prayer life.

Discipline

Your fidelity to this consecration program has required discipline, which will spill over into other areas of your life, improving even your nonreligious activities.

Order

From discipline necessarily follows order. In his *Spiritual Exercises*, Saint Ignatius of Loyola states that exercises such as these help us to bring "order to that which is disordered in our lives."

Interior Peace

Saint Augustine says in his *City of God* that "peace is the tranquility of order." The Holy Spirit is a God of order. Our Lady is the mystical spouse of the Holy Spirit, and devotion to her is producing in your soul interior order that will permeate all other aspects of your life.

Love for Neighbor

By following in the footsteps of our Lady, who went in haste to visit her cousin Elizabeth in the hill country, you have come to see clearly the importance of loving God by means of loving and serving your neighbor. So, too, by following the steps of this consecration program, you have had awakened in your soul apostolic zeal — an ardent desire to serve and help your neighbor, especially on the highway to heaven.

Holiness of Life

There is a simple proverb that says: "Tell me with whom you associate, and I will tell you who you are." As you have spent five weeks in the intimate company of Jesus and Mary — the most holy persons who ever walked the earth — some of their holiness has rubbed off on you.

Improved Sacramental Life

Mary is the Mother of the Church, which feeds and heals you through your sacramental life. As Mary fed Jesus, so you are fed through the Eucharist. Mary has led you to the confessional, where you have been healed through the sacrament of Penance. Deep prayer with Mary has awakened in you the desire for a more frequent and more fervent reception of these sacraments.

Greater Appreciation for the Holy Rosary

Pope Saint John XXIII stated that the Rosary is a summary of the Gospels — in a word, a summary of the life of Jesus and Mary. The saints have strongly recommended the Rosary as a means to conquer the devil, to conquer sin, and for the conversion of sinners. Most important of all, the Blessed Virgin Mary appeared in Fatima six times and each time reminded the children and the world to pray the Rosary.

Finally, the time has come for your consecration

Having spent weeks meditating on the mysteries of the Rosary from the Bible, you can now appreciate much more the beautiful prayer that is the Rosary and Jesus and Mary, whom you have come to know better through those meditations. These meditations should give strength to your resolve as the time comes for you to make your consecration to Jesus through Mary.

With this consecration, Our Lady will grant you special graces to help you live a holy life in your brief time on Earth and to die in God's grace so you can be united with Jesus, Mary, the angels, and the saints for all eternity.

When you are ready, prayerfully make your consecration.

Your Act of Consecration to Jesus through Mary

O eternal and incarnate Wisdom! O sweetest and most adorable Jesus! True God and true man, only Son of the Eternal Father, and of Mary, always virgin! I adore Thee profoundly in the bosom and splendors of Thy Father during eternity; and I adore Thee also in the virginal womb of Mary, Thy most worthy Mother, in the time of Thine Incarnation.

I give Thee thanks that Thou hast annihilated Thyself, taking the form of a slave in order to rescue me from the cruel slavery of the devil. I praise and glorify Thee that Thou hast been pleased to submit Thyself to Mary, Thy holy Mother, in all things, in order to make me Thy faithful slave through her.

But, alas! ungrateful and faithless as I have been, I have not kept the promises that I made so solemnly to Thee in my Baptism; I have not fulfilled my obligations; I do not deserve to be called Thy child, nor yet Thy slave. And as there is nothing in me that does not merit Thine anger and Thy repulse, I dare not come by myself before Thy most holy and august majesty. It is on this account that I have recourse to the intercession of Thy most holy Mother, whom Thou hast given me for a mediatrix with Thee. It is through her that I hope to obtain of Thee contrition, the pardon of my sins, and the acquisition and preservation of wisdom.

Hail, then, O immaculate Mary, living tabernacle of the Divinity, where the Eternal Wisdom willed to be hidden and to be adored by angels and by men! Hail, O Queen of Heaven and Earth, to whose empire everything that is under God is subject. Hail, O sure refuge of sinners, whose mercy fails no one. Hear my desires for Divine Wisdom; and for that end receive the vows and offerings that in my lowliness I present to thee.

TOTAL CONSECRATION

I, _____, a faithless sinner, renew and ratify today in thy hands the vows of my Baptism; I renounce forever Satan, his pomps, and his works; and I give myself entirely to Jesus Christ, the Incarnate Wisdom, to carry my cross after Him all the days of my life, and to be more faithful to Him than I have ever been before.

In the presence of all the heavenly court, I choose thee this day for my Mother and Mistress. I deliver and consecrate to thee, as thy slave, my body and soul, my goods, both interior and exterior, and even the value of all my good actions, past, present, and future; leaving to thee the entire and full right of disposing of me, and all that belongs to me, without exception, according to thy good pleasure, for the greater glory of God in time and in eternity.

Receive, O benignant Virgin, this little offering of my slavery, in honor of, and in union with, that subjection that the Eternal Wisdom deigned to have to thy maternity; in homage to the power that both of you have over this poor sinner; and in thanksgiving for the privileges with which the Holy Trinity has favored thee. I declare that I wish henceforth, as thy true slave, to seek thy honor and to obey thee in all things.

O admirable Mother, present me to thy dear Son as His eternal slave, so that, as He has redeemed me by thee, by thee He may receive me!

O Mother of mercy, grant me the grace to obtain the true Wisdom of God; and for that end receive me among those whom thou lovest and teachest, whom thou leadest, nourishest, and protectest as thy children and thy slaves.

O faithful Virgin, make me in all things so perfect a disciple, imitator, and slave of the Incarnate Wisdom, Jesus Christ, thy Son, that I may attain, by thine intercession and by thine example, to the fullness of His age on earth and of His glory in Heaven. Amen.

Signature: _____

Date: _____

About the Author

FR. ED BROOM, O.M.V.

Fr. Ed Broom, O.M.V., had the privilege of being ordained by Pope Saint John Paul II on Trinity Sunday, May 25, 1986. He worked in South America during his first years as a priest and in Los Angeles for the past twenty-three years.

As an Oblate of the Virgin Mary, Fr. Broom is dedicated to giving the *Spiritual Exercises* of Saint Ignatius of Loyola, to promoting Marian devotion and consecration, and to promoting God's infinite mercy through the sacrament of Confession. He strives to preach the word of God through electronic media, including YouTube, Facebook, podcasts, and blog articles in English and Spanish. Fr. Broom is also the author of *From Humdrum to Holy: A Step-by-Step Guide to Living Like a Saint* (Sophia Institute Press, 2016).

Sophia Institute

Sophia Institute is a nonprofit institution that seeks to nurture the spiritual, moral, and cultural life of souls and to spread the Gospel of Christ in conformity with the authentic teachings of the Roman Catholic Church.

Sophia Institute Press fulfills this mission by offering translations, reprints, and new publications that afford readers a rich source of the enduring wisdom of mankind.

Sophia Institute also operates two popular online Catholic resources: CrisisMagazine.com and CatholicExchange.com.

Crisis Magazine provides insightful cultural analysis that arms readers with the arguments necessary for navigating the ideological and theological minefields of the day. *Catholic Exchange* provides world news from a Catholic perspective as well as daily devotionals and articles that will help you to grow in holiness and live a life consistent with the teachings of the Church.

In 2013, Sophia Institute launched Sophia Institute for Teachers to renew and rebuild Catholic culture through service to Catholic education. With the goal of nurturing the spiritual, moral, and cultural life of souls, and an abiding respect for the role and work of teachers, we strive to provide materials and programs that are at once enlightening to the mind and ennobling to the heart; faithful and complete, as well as useful and practical.

Sophia Institute gratefully recognizes the Solidarity Association for preserving and encouraging the growth of our apostolate over the course of many years. Without their generous and timely support, this book would not be in your hands.

www.SophiaInstitute.com
www.CatholicExchange.com
www.CrisisMagazine.com
www.SophiaInstituteforTeachers.org

Sophia Institute Press® is a registered trademark of Sophia Institute.
Sophia Institute is a tax-exempt institution as defined by the
Internal Revenue Code, Section 501(c)(3). Tax I.D. 22-2548708.